FROM THE TOP DOWN

The Executive Role in

Volunteer Program Success

SUSAN J. ELLIS

With special sections on
accounting issues by John Paul Dalsimer, CPA
and legal questions by Jeffrey D. Kahn, JD

For many years now volunteerism has been my major professional focus. I am deeply committed to making the contributions of volunteers more visible and appreciated. From the Top Down *is directed at an important new audience, in the hope that the chief executives who read these pages come away with a renewed respect for volunteers and the people who lead them—a respect that translates into daily support and wider vision about the potential impact of volunteer efforts.*

No book ever springs full grown from the mind of an author. Rather, it evolves slowly from research, personal experience, innumerable conversations, and lots of listening to the concerns of others. The participants in the workshops I have conducted these past years will never know how their various questions sparked ideas that found their way into the following pages—thank you! I am grateful to the many people who, in one way or another, contributed to the content of this book. Special and warm thanks go to Katherine Noyes for her wise editing and helpful suggestions, to Jeffrey Kahn for his legal perspective and editing help, to Laurence Manou for his graphics and book design, to Paul Brazina, CPA, for his added accounting knowledge, and to Ann Ellis for her loving proofreading and advice.

Printed by
The Kingswood Group, Ardmore, Pennsylvania

Published by
Energize, Inc.
5450 Wissahickon Avenue
Philadelphia, Pennsylvania 19144

CONTENTS

INTRODUCTION

Most books and articles about volunteer program management are designed for the direct supervisor of volunteers. Such frontline managers are the usual audience in the more than 750 training workshops Energize Associates has conducted across the country since 1977. Our workshops (as well as individualized consultation sessions) deal with all aspects of how to start, maintain, or expand the utilization of volunteers in organizations that range from hospitals to courts to museums to schools. The skills of volunteer administration are generic and apply to all settings. After years of training and consulting with so many leaders of volunteers, I have become convinced that many of their concerns stem directly from a lack of substantive support from their agencies' top administrators. This lack of support is not due to malice or unwillingness to be of help, but is rather due to the failure of executives to understand what is really needed from them.

That is why this book has been written for *top level executives* of agencies which already involve volunteers or which are considering starting a volunteer program. Very little has been published previously about the volunteer-related issues that deserve executive attention. It is probably an accurate assumption that most executives were not taught anything about volunteers in their formal schooling. There may have been some time spent on the interrelationship of executives with their boards of directors, which is one aspect of working successfully with volunteers, but few management texts or lecturers speak to the specific issues that will be raised in these pages.

Many volunteer programs suffer from "benign neglect." Only if and when something goes wrong does the executive become involved. Too few CEOs monitor the day-to-day progress of the volunteer program or give the director of volunteers the benefit of ongoing suggestions or input from the administrative perspective. Some executives view volunteers as a "nice" thing to have—"auxiliary" in all the diminutive connotations of that word—but not necessarily as something requiring much management attention.

What a mistake! Perhaps the worst result is that too many volunteer programs languish from a lack of *expectations*—limited vision that stops volunteers from achieving their fullest impact or productivity. The unfortunate fact is that more volunteers are *underutilized* than are overburdened.

The target audience of this book is the top decision-maker. You might be the executive director of a nonprofit agency or its board president; you might be the CEO of a large institution, whether profit-making or not; or you might be the director of a government agency. While some of the issues presented here may differ for the specifics or size of your particular setting, there are really more similarities than differences between the types of organizations that utilize volunteers.

Your organization may have no volunteers at present or may already benefit from a large, well-established volunteer corps. It is never too soon nor too late to examine the concerns outlined in the following pages.

You may be seeking volunteers who are specialists in specific fields or those who are generalists—or both. The types of assignments your organization offers to volunteers may range from long-term, ongoing work to one-time special events; some may need to be done on-site in your facility, while other assignments may involve independent work in the community. You may call volunteer work by labels such as "citizen participation," "public service," "internships," "community involvement," "self-help," or *pro bono publico* work. Regardless of the scope, diversity, or vocabulary of the volunteer program you plan, the basic principles discussed here will apply.

This book is not meant to be a distillation of all the resources available on how to develop and manage a volunteer program. Whomever you designate to direct volunteers is encouraged to seek out those resources and learn more about the details of effective, daily volunteer administration. Rather, this book deals with issues that are directly in your control as the executive. It is also designed to be thought-provoking and provide you with a basis upon which to make necessary decisions.

Some of the concepts proposed in the following pages may seem radical. Actually, there is a fair mix of suggestions based on time-proven principles and of proposals articulated in print for the first time. In order to stimulate and stretch perspectives, however, I present the most logical extension of the way the best volunteer programs operate. You are free, of course, to pick and choose among the recommendations here to develop the form of volunteer administration that will meet your own organization's needs.

Some readers may be feeling a bit uncomfortable in the suspicion that I am going to suggest lots of structure to bureaucratize volunteerism. The fact is that successful volunteering does not come from spontaneous combustion. Most of our organizations today are already rather complex and, unless we develop clear ways for volunteers to participate in our activities, people really do not know how to become involved. This is true whether the organization is an "agency," an "institution," or an all-volunteer association.

It is also important to avoid wasting the time of volunteers—which is exactly what happens if there has been insufficient planning to define and prepare the work to be done. It is a form of volunteer recognition to establish standards for who can become a volunteer, how assignments are made, and whether accomplishments will be evaluated. The best volunteer program management serves to *enable* volunteer achievement, not limit it.

All the management principles that work effectively with employees apply equally to volunteers. But surprisingly enough, the theme of this book is not necessarily to treat volunteers in the same way you would treat salaried staff. Volunteer administration emphasizes motivators such as choice, positive working environment, and recognition, to which all workers will respond with increased morale and productivity. So, this book proposes that it may be better management practice to *treat salaried staff as though they were volunteers!*

The first step to volunteer program success is *vision*. Volunteers can expand the horizons of your organization and your staff. Encourage volunteers to be creative and innovative partners in service delivery, and then expect the best. Self-fulfilling prophecy is a key factor. If your concept of what volunteers can contribute is limited, you will design a volunteer program structure that indeed keeps achievement low. But if you are open to the potential of what might develop, you will find ways to encourage volunteers' success.

The second step is *commitment.* You must have the conviction that volunteers are important . . . that they are the "nonsalaried personnel" of the agency. Volunteers are not "added spice" to your organizational mix. Instead, they are one of the main ingredients. As top executive, you can establish and enforce this premise throughout your organization.

As we will examine in the next chapter, it is important to have a clear understanding of why volunteers are valuable in your setting. Articulating the reasons for involving volunteers is an executive level responsibility . . . and it forms the foundation on which your organization will build its volunteer participation.

WHY VOLUNTEERS?

When Energize Associates conducts training seminars, we often include a session to examine and articulate the underlying assumptions of volunteer involvement. We present a list of key questions all leaders of volunteers should go home and ask—regardless of how old or new their volunteer program is. The first—and most critical—question is: "*Why* do we want volunteers?" This question is absolutely basic, yet it catches some people by surprise. Isn't the answer obvious? No. Aren't agencies "supposed" to have volunteers? Not necessarily. Hasn't our organization "always had" volunteers? So what?

As the executive, why *do* you want volunteers? Well, one answer always seems to be: "because we do not have sufficient resources (money, staff, or whatever) to do our job without the help of volunteers." Unfortunately, while this response may be accurate, it also is a rather negative statement about volunteers. The implied corollary is that *if* there was sufficient money, or staff, or whatever, then volunteers would *not* be necessary. This makes volunteers a *second choice* resource.

I submit that this reasoning is at the root of a lot of the problems agencies have in activating volunteers and in working successfully with them. Recruitment based on "we don't have enough resources, so we are forced to turn to you" is not positive. Neither is supervision by salaried staff based on "I wish I had a paid helper, but I have to settle for you."

There are indeed some *first choice* reasons for wanting to attract volunteers—reasons that have nothing to do with the presence or absence of money. In our workshops, we ask trainees to imagine a "utopia" in which organizations such as theirs would have all the money in the world with which to do anything they please: offer one-to-one client service, pay for all types of consultation, take the staff on a retreat to Bermuda, etc. Here is the "exercise" question we pose: given such a "utopia," would your agency still utilize volunteers in some way?

It generally takes several minutes for participants to be able to sort out their reactions to this question. And they find it hard to answer, at least at first. Some people honestly admit—with some relief—that they would not involve volunteers anymore. Others get sidetracked in observing that some people would still want to offer their services *as* volunteers—but we quickly point out that just because some people would always want to *be* volunteers does not mean that every agency would have to create an assignment for them. So the exercise has to take the *agency's* perspective only.

First Choice Reasons   After some lively discussion, the following are finally identified as being the unique things volunteers offer an organization—so special to volunteers that paying a salary negates or changes them completely:

- Volunteers have **credibility because they are unsalaried.** Paid staff are always perceived as "spokespeople" with a degree of *vested interest* in the outcome of a legislative hearing or funding proposal, since their livelihood depends upon the outcome. Volunteers, because their motivation is not profit-oriented, are seen by donors, clients, legislators, and the public as more objective and even as more sincere. This is what makes them such a public relations asset.

  Note that this perception of volunteers as having no vested interest sometimes has nothing to do with the truth. For example, if a volunteer's grandmother founded the organization, then s/he has a different form of "vested interest"! Also, if s/he has been on the board for 20 years, objectivity may be questionable. But the fact remains that the *perception and assumption* of the listener or recipient are that the volunteer is more credible.

- Another version of this is that receiving assistance from a volunteer (rather than from a salaried staff member) **makes a difference to the recipient.** Many consumers are distrustful of salaried service providers and are there-fore more likely to believe and follow a volunteer's suggestions.

  In some circumstances, the important factor is the feeling that the volunteer is doing the task willingly—voluntarily—while the salaried staff are simply "doing a job." This is why prisoners, for example, are more will-ing to talk with volunteer visitors than with guards or state social workers. It is why patients in hospitals are more cheered by the visit of a volunteer than a nurse: volunteers demonstrate that neighbors have not forgotten them nor are "turned off" by their illness. Nurses, on the other hand, must provide service, regardless of their per-sonal feelings about the patient.

  Finally, some programs such as one-to-one home visitation or Big Brothers/Big Sisters would change radi-cally in their purpose without volunteers. If we salary a Big Brother, we give the child another babysitter. The very word "brother" in the volunteer's title indicates that the service is not based on its being a "job." The same idea is at work with the title of "friendly visitor."

- Volunteers are valuable as **objective policy makers** and would therefore still be involved as members of boards of directors. Since the ultimate power of a board is to close the agency, it is clear that such decision-making should be done by people who are not personally affected by such an action nor by less drastic measures such as cutting some programs, etc. Also, the objectivity of volunteers is aided by not being on-site full time. Dis-tance provides perspective.

- Volunteers are more **free to criticize** than are salaried staff. Again, this is a function of being outside the career-ladder, promotion-seeking concerns that are often legiti-mate for the salaried staff.

- Because volunteers are not dependent upon the organization for their livelihood, they can approach assignments with **less pressure** and stress, often an asset in accomplishing the tasks to be done.

- Because volunteers are always **"private citizens,"** they are free to contact legislators, newspapers, etc. in a way the salaried staff may not be permitted to do (because of possible limitations on legislative activity by such regulations as the Hatch Act). Though this is a two-edged sword (i.e., the volunteer may use this access to speak against you), it means that volunteers can be powerful advocates. Similarly, though volunteers act as "agents" of your organization, they have more flexibility in cutting through some of the red tape of bureaucratic systems, political boundaries, and other artificial barriers.

- Volunteers can **experiment** with new ideas and service approaches that are not yet ready to be funded—or that no one wants to fund for a wide variety of reasons. Historically, in fact, volunteers have always been the pioneers in creating new services, often against the tide of more traditional institutions.

Implications   What does all this imply? Well, first it shows that there are definitely areas in which volunteers—*because they are volunteers*—can be even more effective than salaried staff. Second it raises the question of whether your agency is maximizing these "first choice" areas. Specifically, in your organization:

—are volunteers being used as legislative advocates? as fundraisers? as public educators? in any role that makes use of their credibility?

—are volunteers providing direct service to consumers, especially in tasks that may benefit from a higher degree of comfort level or personalization?

—do you have a system for getting feedback from volunteers? are there channels for making suggestions or stating criticisms?

—do you utilize volunteers to establish collaborative arrangements or to cut red tape in some way?

Examine the job descriptions volunteers are presently fulfilling in your setting and determine whether you are benefitting as much as possible from the unique aspects of volunteer service.

So Why Pay a Salary?

Perhaps you have been thinking about the reverse of the question of why you involve volunteers, namely: "why should we salary anyone?" It is important (especially for this book) to recognize that the answer is *not* that offering a salary gets you people with better *qualifications.* A volunteer can be just as highly trained and experienced as can any employee. Instead, offering a salary gives the agency a **pre-determined number of work hours** per week, **the right to dictate the employee's work schedule,** a certain amount of **control** over the nature and priorities of the work to be done, and **continuity.**

When you pay a salary, you can require that the person give your organization 40 hours a week or whatever number is necessary. Because most people need to earn a living, people can rarely give one agency that much volunteer time per week.

In addition, volunteers are always free to select their individual work schedule. Though you can require volunteers to commit to a schedule and be dependable, a person does not usually jeopardize his/her volunteer position by telling you up front that s/he goes to Florida in February or that his/her schedule will change every semester to match a course roster. On the other hand, an employee can indeed be told exactly when the agency expects him or her to be present and can be made to submit vacation schedules, for example, for prior approval.

The area of "control" has many levels and will be discussed in more detail in Chapter 9. Some of what you may feel you have in the way of control over salaried staff may be more mythical than real. For example, you really have no way of stopping an employee from going to the press with a story—though you can threaten termination of employment and hope the fear of being fired is a deterrent. The more realistic aspect of control is that you can dictate job assignments and expect the employee to fulfill these, even if s/he dislikes the task or even disagrees with it. Further, you can set the priorities within which the employee must emphasize certain tasks over others. A volunteer always retains *freedom of choice* and can refuse to work on a project for various reasons, without losing the opportunity to volunteer in another assignment.

Finally, a salaried position provides continuity for the organization. Even if the person filling the position changes over time, the function itself remains relatively stable. The public and the rest of staff can expect a certain standard in the way the service is provided by that position.

Other Benefits of Volunteers

As we have seen, there are some clear "first choice" reasons for utilizing volunteers, even in an all-the-money-in-the-world utopia. And there are good reasons for salarying some workers, too. Since we live in the real, limited resources world, what are the other benefits to an organization for involving volunteers? Volunteers offer:

- Extra hands and the potential to do more than could be done simply with limited salaried staff; this "more" might mean an increased amount of service, expanded hours of operation, or different/new types of services.

- Diversity; volunteers may be different from the salaried staff in terms of age, race, social background, income, educational level, etc. This translates into many more points of view and perhaps even a sort of checks and balances to the danger of the staff becoming myopic or inbred.

- Skills that augment the ones salaried staff already possess. Ideally volunteers are recruited exactly because the salaried staff cannot have every skill or talent necessary to do all aspects of the job. These skills can be very concrete such as being bilingual, knowing how to dry herbs, or being able to produce a newsletter. Or, they can be less tangible such as being able to relate to teenagers or the disabled.

- Access to the community, because most volunteers live nearby (as does the salaried staff, but their credibility is often less than volunteers, as we've already noted). This also means good public relations, in that happy volunteers will speak well of the organization to their neighbors. Here is another two-edged sword, of course, because unhappy volunteers can create bad will for you, too.

- The option to focus intensively on a particular issue or client, even to the exclusion of everything else. This is a luxury of concentration and time not normally justifiable for the salaried staff, while volunteers can actually be recruited to provide such individualized attention.

In addition to all of the above, studies have shown that satisfied volunteers frequently are so supportive of the organizations with which they serve that they become donors of money and goods as well. They also support special events and fundraisers by attending themselves and bringing along family and friends. In the case of cultural arts organizations, volunteers thereby help to expand the audience or public for performances and exhibitions.

As you begin or expand your orga-nization's volunteer component you (or your director of volunteers) will be assessing the needs that vol-

Putting These Benefits to Work

unteers might fill. Being clear on why you want volunteer involvement (the benefits we have just listed) will help to identify specific volunteer job descriptions.

The wrong question to ask when trying to define volunteer assignments is: "what could a volunteer do to help us?" The answer is generally tainted by the staff's (and your) stereotypes about who might be recruited. If you envision a little old lady in a flowered hat and tennis shoes, then you will give a very limited response to the question of what such a volunteer could do for you!

Therefore, the more meaningful question is: "what needs to be done?" This has some sub-categories, such as:

—what are we doing now that we would like to do more of?

—what unmet needs do our clients have that we presently can do nothing about?

—what unmet needs does the staff have (to support them in their work)?

—what might we do differently if we had more skills or time available to us?

The answers to these questions will provide a wide range of possible assignments. Not every idea will be appropriate to implement with a volunteer, but the door will be open to creative and challenging assignments.

As CEO, you have a role to play in making sure that salaried staff brainstorm creatively in finding ways for volunteers to become involved. Help employees avoid "dumping" on volunteers all the tasks they find distasteful or low level. While it is wonderful if a volunteer can be recruited who enjoys the things the employee dislikes, thereby pleasing them both, this approach backfires if the employee never intends to share any of the tasks that are more challenging or rewarding.

Once you have a sense of the kinds of needs you want volunteers to meet, you are ready to consider the practical aspects of implementing a volunteer program.

CONSIDERATIONS
IN PLANNING

From the perspective of human resource management, it is clear that the volunteer program is the nonsalaried personnel department of the agency. What does this mean in practice?

If you were given a donation today for $100,000, with the stipulation that it be spent on salaries for new employees, you would know exactly how to proceed effectively. You would probably follow a sequence of tasks very much like this:

—assess the agency's needs and pinpoint where new employees would be most useful;

—develop job descriptions, including the qualifications you'd look for in applicants;

—publicize the openings;

—interview and screen applicants, with the expectation that you will have to turn away some candidates in your search for the best people;

—select the people you will hire and match them to the available openings;

—orient these new employees to the policies and practices of the agency;

—train these new employees in the specifics of the job to which each has been assigned.

Once the new employees were on board, you would then be concerned about their supervision, in-service training, and periodic performance evaluation. As top administrator, you'd recognize that if any one of these personnel management steps is omitted or done without high standards, effective, quality delivery of service is jeopardized.

The premise of this book is that every one of these tasks is equally pertinent to the effective utilization of *volunteers*. If you accept this premise, the following are ways to plan for the integration of volunteers into your organization.

Statement of Philosophy

We have already considered the question of "why do we want volunteers?" Once you have identified exactly why *your* organization wishes to involve volunteers, it is very helpful to develop a written "Statement of Philosophy" expressing your point of view. This statement can be useful in a number of ways, especially for establishing clear relationships between volunteers and salaried staff, for recruiting new volunteers, and for demonstrating appreciation of citizen involvement. The Statement of Philosophy then becomes the basis or framework upon which you and the board of directors can develop goals, policies and other decisions affecting volunteers in the organization.

When drafting a Statement of Philosophy, it is important to be specific about why you are involving volunteers. For example, a statement that says only, "volunteers will assist in the achievement of agency goals," is insufficient. Similarly, a statement that limits roles, such as "volunteers will supplement, not supplant, paid staff" also does not do the trick. Though this latter sentiment has been gospel in some quarters, it is also limiting. For example, why must volunteers only "supplement"? Why can't they "innovate," or "experiment," or "work parallel to"? None of these roles diminish the importance of the function of the salaried staff.

A better approach to the Statement of Philosophy would be something like this:

> *Our agency encourages the teamwork of salaried staff and volunteers so that we can offer our consumers the best services possible. Volunteers contribute their unique talents, skills, and knowledge of our community to provide person-*

*alized attention to consumers, enable the salaried staff to
concentrate on the work for which they were trained, and
educate the public about our organization and its cause.*

In a government agency (whether national, state or local),
the role of "citizen participation" deserves clarification in such a
Statement of Philosophy. Here is one way to express political commitment to teamwork between civil servants and citizen
volunteers.

In a residential facility such as a nursing home, the Statement of Philosophy could include something about the interrelationship of the volunteers, salaried staff, and the residents themselves. For example, you might state the desire of the agency to
encourage residents to participate fully in the activities that create
a home environment for all residents.

It should come as no surprise that   **Goals and**
good volunteer management   **Objectives**
requires the setting of goals and
objectives for the achievements of
the volunteer program. There is no reason to let abounding gratitude for donated volunteer time restrain an organization from setting standards of achievement. In fact, volunteers usually prefer to
have some way to assess their service contribution.

In developing initial and then ongoing goals and objectives,
bigger is not always better. There are other ways to measure the
successful impact of volunteers than to point to having "more"
volunteers this year than last year. The simple addition of more
people into the volunteer program does not self-evidently mean
better service delivery. Numerical goals of "how many" volunteers to bring on board are meaningless unless serious expectations of productivity are also articulated. Just as with employees, it
is possible to monitor and measure the accomplishments of volunteers by stating goals and objectives at the beginning of a period—
and then assessing whether these were achieved.

In formulating goals and objectives for the volunteer program, you might consider such questions as:

—What do we expect individual volunteers to accomplish
   in each job category?

—What type of diversity do we want represented in our volunteer program?

—What reaction do we want our consumers to have to the service they receive from volunteers?

—What effect do we want volunteers to have in special assignments, such as public education, public relations, etc.?

—What outreach efforts do we expect our director of volunteers to make this year?

Goals and objectives set for the volunteer component should correlate with the overall goals and objectives of the agency. Remember to include volunteers in your plans for future agency projects. If, for example, you are proposing a new community outreach effort that will be under the auspices of the public relations department, and you expect to train volunteers as speakers in that effort, develop a written objective for this. After all, if you wanted the community outreach project to develop a film, you would certainly include an objective relating to the work of the audiovisual department. As CEO, you have the responsibility for inserting an objective relating to volunteer utilization into the plans for any appropriate project and, as we will discuss later, for involving the person in charge of the volunteer program in such overall agency planning.

Policy Setting

Throughout this book you will recognize issues that can be solved or avoided by setting policy in advance that everyone understands. Since you and the board of directors (volunteers themselves, of course) are responsible for developing and implementing policy, you have the authority to set the rules for volunteer involvement. When people understand the rules, they can either follow them or work to change them. But without rules in place, everyone operates independently—and you have no way of enforcing standards.

Each of the chapters in this book suggests an area requiring policy decisions. It is a policy decision to recruit volunteers in the first place, and to allocate resources to their support. Make the effort to identify existing policy gaps, especially in terms of the interaction between volunteers and salaried staff. Be sure all new (and veteran) employees know the standards you have set and be alert to new situations which require revision of policies about volunteers.

The setting—and then the enforcing—of policies involving volunteers are two of the most visible ways you can demonstrate commitment to the integration of volunteers into your organization.

Where You Are Now

As already indicated, you may be the executive of an organization at any stage of its volunteer program development. However, you may find yourself wanting to fill in the planning gaps overlooked in the past. If you already have volunteers on site, be sure to involve them as much as possible in helping to define their situation. Forming an ad hoc planning team of current volunteers may be one way to do some of the work necessary to define the program structure. Such a team also allows volunteers genuine participation in the program. After all, you are formulating policies and procedures that will affect them (and may change some of the ways they operate now). What better way to show that you, as CEO, value volunteer input than to ask them for advice?

If you have decided to involve volunteers for the first time, analyze your organization to see if "bootlegged" volunteers are already active. For example, have you been asking neighboring church groups to help you once a year with a special event? Are friends and relatives of service recipients (or the board, or the staff) allowed to "help out" if they are interested? Are students given the chance to do internships? You may discover that you already have quite a list of "volunteers," though you may not have identified them as such in the past. You need to know if you are starting from scratch or indeed have a base of community supporters upon which to build. This identification process can be pleasantly revealing.

Starting Small

No matter what your ultimate goals for volunteer involvement are, it is good management practice to start small. Pilot test new volunteer assignment categories, allowing time to work out the procedural details that will only surface once a volunteer is on the job. Give salaried staff the chance to learn how to work successfully with volunteers and add more people only as the support structure develops.

Perhaps you can select one or two units of the agency in which to begin placing volunteers, expanding to the other units over time.

Management Options

Each reader will come to this book under different circumstances. You may be operating in an agency in which there is already a highly-structured and well-managed volunteer component, or you may be considering starting a volunteer program for the first time. You may be the head of a large institution or the only salaried staff member among a multitude of volunteers. Whatever your situation, you will have to make some choices as to how you wish to begin or continue involving volunteers. Some management options are:

Model I: You, as head of the organization, lead the volunteer program and personally supervise volunteers just as you do paid staff.

Model II: You designate a leader for the volunteer "program" and all volunteers are recruited and supervised by this "Director of Volunteers."

Model III: The volunteer program is "decentralized," in that all staff recruit and supervise volunteers active in their particular units.

Model IV: A mixture of models II and III, in which you designate a Director of Volunteers who recruits and administers volunteers, but deploys them to whichever units need assistance; day-to-day supervision is given by the line staff.

Model V: Volunteers are self-led, generally organized with elected officers, etc.

Model IV is the most common management option, but there are still more choices to make in determining the leadership of volunteers. An entire chapter will be devoted to staffing the volunteer program, but your choices are basically two: you designate an existing member of the salaried staff to head the volunteer program in addition to his or her other responsibilities, or, you create a new part-time or full-time employee position of director of volunteers.

Whatever management option you choose, to whom will you have the person in charge of volunteers report? This decision impacts on **Organizational Placement** your entire chain of command and sends a message to all employees and volunteers. In a later chapter, we will consider the question of supervision of the leader of volunteers more fully but, for now, recognize that where you place the head of the program implies where—even whether—volunteers themselves are integrated into the organization.

There is no "correct" place for the director of volunteers on the organizational chart. Each setting is different and parameters such as agency size, job descriptions of other staff members, etc. will affect your decision. However, be aware that whoever supervises the director of volunteers must truly understand the things that make that position unique (see Chapter 4). For example, if you place the volunteer program under the Public Relations Department, will the director of public relations be able to assist the director of volunteers in her/his responsibilities related to the daily operations of the agency? Generally, a PR Department has no role in in-house service delivery or activities. Conversely, if the director of volunteers is placed under, say, the casework supervisor, will that person be supportive of the volunteer program's public outreach efforts? Again, the casework supervisor would normally have no reason to do public speaking, etc.

In reality, the director of volunteers is a *separate, independent department head,* in that s/he has responsibilities substantially different from, though linked to, all other departments, and in that s/he supervises a large cadre of workers, albeit volunteers. Ideally, the director of volunteers should answer directly to you. This also sends a message to *volunteers.* It says that they have a direct line to the top decision maker. It conveys a similar message to all employees: volunteers are a subject of daily interest to the top executive. When you consider that the volunteer program is the agency's nonsalaried personnel department and that you, as CEO, are responsible for the deployment of all human resources, the decision to place the director of volunteers directly under you is more than justifiable.

If you are the executive of a very large organization, the director of volunteers may have to report to you through a vice-president or some other key administrator. Again, recognize the messages you send to everyone through your choice of where to place the volunteer program. Consider the other organizational units answering to the same administrator and assess whether there is an evident rationale for placing the volunteer program alongside these other units—or whether the placement implies that volunteers are a "miscellaneous" agency function.

Organizational Chart

Does your present organizational chart include volunteers? Take out the chart you show to funding sources or to new employees. Are volunteers mentioned on it at all? To begin with, if you are in a voluntary agency, are the members of your board of directors noted? They should be at the top of your hierarchy, shouldn't they? Now what about line volunteers? Advisory committees? Etc.?

The main, and therefore priority, work of each employee is generally reflected on an organizational chart. So if the person responsible for volunteers holds a different title and sees volunteer management as only a small part of his/her job, then it is possible volunteers will be overlooked on the organizational chart. But where does this leave volunteers? Are they invisible?

When an organization has a designated director of volunteers who fills no other function, it is probable that s/he will appear on the chart as an employee. But too often the volunteers s/he leads are not indicated at all. If volunteers themselves do appear on the organizational chart, they sometimes are indicated this way:

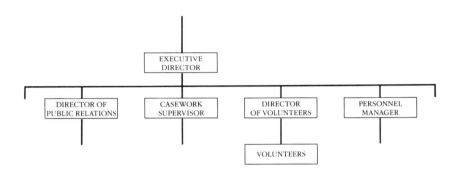

What message does this chart send? It says that volunteers "belong" to the director of volunteers and effectively lets all other salaried staff off the hook in caring about volunteers. Yet if you have a Personnel Department, are all "employees" listed under it? Of course not. Only payroll clerks and others who are directly supervised by the personnel manager are shown "under" him or her, while all other employees are shown under the departments in which they are placed. The Volunteer Department works in exactly the same way—channelling volunteers to the appropriate units where daily supervision is provided. So a more accurate organizational chart might look like the accompanying illustration.

Sometimes CEOs are reluctant to create such an organizational chart in the fear that funding sources will incorrectly surmise that the agency has sufficient resources. It seems somehow dishonest to show so many "staff." One way to handle this to make sure the chart is labelled as a *functioning* organizational

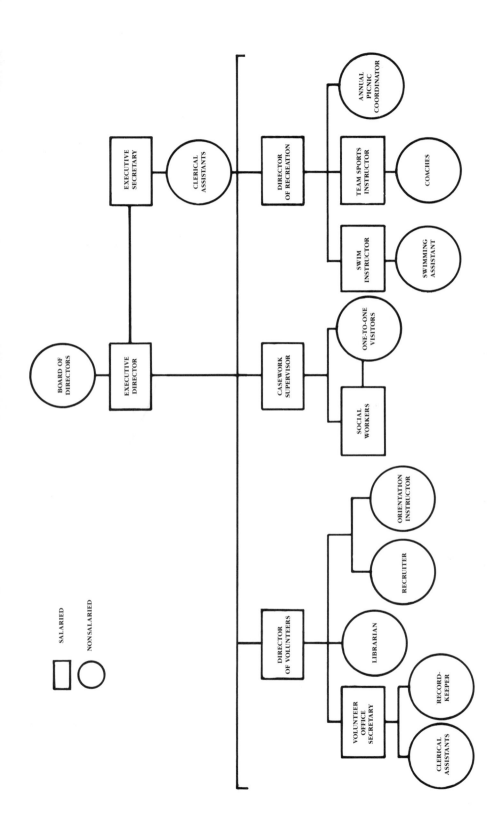

chart, not as simply a list of salaried staff. Then indicate employees by circles or squares, and the volunteers by a differently shaped "box." Or use solid and dotted lines.

One more point: always use *titles* when referring to volunteers—and don't feel that you have to keep the adjective "volunteer" in the title. If a volunteer is coordinating your alumni drive, then s/he is the Alumni Drive Coordinator—does it matter what the salary is or isn't?

Agency Image

One more consideration in planning for volunteers is to be sure your "house is in order" before opening the doors to recruit help from members of the public. While no one expects an organization to function perfectly nor to have superhuman staff members, volunteers are affected by internal agency problems. If the staff squabbles or are disorganized, volunteers will be caught in the middle.

The ability to recruit volunteers is strongly and directly connected to your organization's image in the community. If your services are viewed negatively for any reason, it will be hard to attract good volunteers (though people will respond positively to a request to help make things better). On the other hand, if the public sees your agency effectively filling a need, it will be easier to encourage volunteers to join you.

Having *no* image or visibility in the community poses similar recruitment problems. If people are unclear about what it is you do (which might be furthered by a confusing agency name), then you or your leader of volunteers will first have to conduct a generalized public relations effort before you can concentrate on the specifics of volunteer recruitment. After all, how can someone be expected to offer you service if s/he doesn't know what you do?

Backing Up the Plan

In this chapter we have examined areas requiring thoughtful planning and preparation. In the next chapter we'll talk about money. Successful volunteer involvement necessitates not only the allocating of funds, but also providing access to other organizational resources.

BUDGETING AND
ALLOCATING RESOURCES

Volunteers are not "free" labor. They are a human resource that costs substantially less in hard cash than any other resource, but funds, space, supplies and other materials must be allocated to support the work of volunteers. The "cost effectiveness" of such allocations is easy to prove: the expenses incurred by a volunteer component are "leverage" money that translates into contribution of services valued at many multiples of the original expenditure. Later, we'll look at what that value of volunteer service really is— and how to compute it.

Avoid the mistake of seeing the volunteer program as "small" simply because there are few salaried staff assigned to it. Though personnel costs may be low, the volunteer program's budget needs in other categories can be substantial because of the additional people being put to work.

Let's examine each possible line item in a volunteer program budget and discuss the considerations in arriving at a reasonable dollar figure. Special needs in the start-up phase of a program will be indicated in each category.

PERSONNEL

As you review the expenditures necessary in the personnel category, consider both direct and indirect costs. As we will be discussing in the chapter on staffing, the number of full or part-time staff you designate or hire will depend upon many factors, including the number and types of volunteers in the program, hours of operation, etc. Determining the salary of the director of volunteers should be based on the following criterion:

What are you presently paying other department heads or key administrative employees?

The director of volunteers is not a low-level position. It certainly is not a clerical function nor is it line supervision. The job requires decision-making, leadership, and a great deal of public contact on behalf of the agency. You should therefore budget for the position on the basis of its professional demands—and hire accordingly!

The personnel budget category will, of course, include the program's secretary and any additional assistants necessary because of the size or schedule of the program. Employee benefits are the next line item.

You might want to estimate the cost of the time devoted by other agency staff to the training and supervision of volunteers. While this will not be a direct budget line item, it may help you in identifying the true value of the resources you are allocating to supporting volunteers.

OPERATIONAL COSTS AND OTHER NEEDED RESOURCES

Several of the following items will not be new expenses but will require a re-allocation of organizational resources.

Space and Other Facilities

The volunteer program needs office space that affords the following:

—Easy access from the entrance of the building, since prospective volunteers (members of the public) will be coming in for interviews. Also, proximity to the entrance will allow the director of volunteers to maintain contact with volunteers arriving and departing on their scheduled work days (e.g., permitting control of the sign in/out system, etc.).

—Privacy for interviewing prospective volunteers.

—Secure storage space for volunteers' coats and other personal belongings (and uniforms, if applicable).

—Group work space to permit meetings, collating of materials, etc.

In addition to the space needed on a daily basis, the volunteer office also needs *access* to:

—Space for orientation sessions and in-service training meetings (varying group sizes).

—Adequate rest room facilities. (Remember, the numbers of volunteers that may enter the building daily may be high enough to put a strain on your existing facilities. The school system in Anchorage, Alaska faced this exact problem when teachers in hurriedly-erected "Quonset hut" elementary school buildings refused to allow volunteers to utilize the toilets in the "faculty lounges." It turned out that these lounges only contained "one-seaters" and that an extra 20 or so adults per day genuinely caused a rest room line for the teachers. This is a great example of lack of *planning!)*

—Space in various locations for sign-in books or other volunteer communication mechanisms, such as bulletin boards.

—Possibly, lounge areas for volunteer rest periods.

It is not always stating the obvious to note that each volunteer also needs adequate space in which to work. Staff may indeed want assistance with a variety of projects, but has anyone thought through *where* the volunteer will sit, have a clear surface, etc.? Also, is there anywhere that the volunteer can *store* his or her work in-between visits? Is there any provision for a mail bin or file folder so that messages may be left for the volunteer? These kinds of details make work go smoothly and indicate that volunteers are indeed integrated into the organizational environment.

Furniture and Equipment

Assess available work space and furniture in terms of the impact of more people (volunteers) coming into the facility at various hours.

Too many organizations have discovered too late that they did not have enough *chairs* for volunteers who dutifully arrived for work at their scheduled time.

Other needs (most of which are clearly one-time costs rather than annual expenses) are:

—coat racks

—typewriters (especially if a number of volunteers have been recruited to do clerical work—salaried secretaries usually do not like to share their typewriters, which may not be feasible anyway due to the placement of typing desks)

—slide projector and screen (for recruitment or volunteer orientation slide shows, etc.)

—bulletin boards

—file cabinets (keep in mind that the volunteer office is the nonsalaried *personnel* office and will generate files in much the same way as the employee personnel office does)

—possibly some comfortable furniture for a conversation/ interview or lounge area

Telephone

Again, the number of telephone instruments and lines will depend upon the size and nature of volunteer activities. But keep in mind that the volunteer office depends heavily on telephone contacts— both in recruitment/public relations and in ongoing communication with volunteers.

If you are creating any project that involves telephoning *by volunteers*—telephone reassurance programs, market surveying, political canvassing, client follow-up, etc.—the possible rise in cost of telephone calls may be a major consideration for you. With the changes in telephone company service still evolving, the budget line for telephone calls may increase in the future, even if local calls form the bulk of the contacts.

Supplies

This is a budget category that is too often treated as minor, while it is really the tip of an iceberg. Budgeting for supplies should be done on the basis of the needs of both the volunteer "office" and the volunteers themselves. Consumption of supplies will rise as the number of active volunteers increases—productivity comes at the cost of support materials. A possible list of supplies would include:

> —paper and stationery
> —pencils and pens
> —typewriter ribbons and similar supplies
> —paper clips, erasers, etc.
> —paper towels and other maintenance materials
> —coffee, tea, and paper cups

In one of the workshops I ran for school principals, a participant asked to address his colleagues. He proceeded to tell the true story of his experience in the first year of inviting volunteers into his school. In the March faculty meeting, he admonished his teachers for having wastefully depleted the school's supply of ditto paper. Came the response: "but now, with all the volunteers, we have been able to give the pupils a chance for individual study exercises, so we've been running off ditto masters in larger numbers than ever before." So the principal wanted to advise his colleagues: "If you're going to start having volunteers, you'd better increase your paper supply requisition." What excellent, practical advice!

One way to estimate your costs for supplies might be to translate the cumulative number of hours served by volunteers (or anticipated being served) annually into "full-time equivalent" (FTE) staff positions. For example, if an employee works 2,080 hours a year (40 hours per week x 52), then a volunteer program logging 10,000 hours of volunteer service per year can be said to give the organization the equivalent of 4.8 full-time employee hours of service—4.8 FTE. If you normally budget supplies using a formula of $xx per employee, to arrive at the supply budget for the volunteer program, simply take $xx and multiply it times the total of the number of salaried staff *and* the FTE number of volunteer staff.[1]

Printing and Reproduction

This is a major line item for a volunteer program, especially in the first year. The following items all require printing or photocopying:

—volunteer application forms and other recordkeeping forms
—recruitment brochures, flyers, posters, mailings, and other tools
—recognition certificates, invitations, etc.
—possibly a volunteer newsletter (quarterly?)
—perhaps a volunteer handbook or manual (in the second year?)
—training materials

Postage

The amount necessary for postage will depend, of course, on such variables as whether the volunteer program mails a volunteer newsletter or intends to use mass mailings of any sort to recruit volunteers.

Insurance

The whole issue of insurance will be discussed later in this book. Suffice it to say here that the cost of accident and/or liability insurance for volunteers may have to be a budget item if your existing insurance package does not already accommodate volunteers. Supplementary automobile insurance may also be a need, if some volunteers are utilized as drivers for your organization. Special, one-time event insurance may also be necessary if the volunteers run major fundraising extravaganzas for you.

First talk to your present insurance carrier, but be aware that special programs designed specifically for coverage of volunteer insurance needs are available at reasonable cost. (See Chapter 9 and Appendix B.)

Recognition

Though it is optional to budget for a major volunteer recognition event such as a party or a dinner, some consideration should be given to how the organization will say thank you to volunteers (and perhaps also to the staff who supervise them). Certificates of appreciation are not expensive, while gift items can be budgeted at a wide range of cost. Even a minimal amount of money can permit an enjoyable recognition event—punch and cookies can show appreciation as well as a steak dinner can.

"Enabling" funds are reimburse-   **Enabling Funds**
ment given to volunteers for out-of-
pocket expenses incurred in the
course of volunteer service. This is
meant to "enable" people to give their services freely, especially if the cost of volunteering would otherwise prohibit some people from participating. The concept of enabling funds is comparatively new to the world of volunteerism and stems from the desire to diversify the corps of volunteers as much as possible. If consideration is not given to out-of-pocket costs, then too many programs will have as volunteers only those people who can afford the "luxury" of volunteering. People on fixed incomes, students with little outside income, and low-income people will otherwise be shut out of the opportunity to give their time and energy to causes that they care about.

Some agencies are able to provide in-kind support of volunteers through existing resources, as opposed to having to budget funds to reimburse cash expenditures. Items offered by such agencies include:

—parking lot privileges or van transportation
—meals on site
—free uniforms or uniform cleaning services
—refreshments, such as hot or cold drinks
—access to an agency-run child care service

When an organization can indeed offer these types of items to volunteers, they might be budgeted under the heading of "benefits" and certainly should be described as such in recruitment materials.

If your agency does not have the option of offering such benefits as in-kind, consider the types of items that cost volunteers money and therefore might be reimbursed by the organization, such as:

—transportation to/from the assignment
—child care costs
—telephone or postage costs for work done at home
—special clothing needs (aprons, work gloves, etc.)
—money spent directly on clients, such as taking a child to
    a movie or buying supplies for an art class

Some agencies offer reimbursement to volunteers on the basis of economic need. Clearly this is a tricky area and requires thoughtful procedures to encourage volunteers to identify their expenses. Philosophically, I believe in offering reimbursement to *every* volunteer and then allowing those who prefer to expend the money as a donation to say so.

Volunteer expenses should be budgeted visibly to acknowledge their existence. If some (even most) volunteers select to donate these costs to the agency, this can be shown as "revenue" to offset the "expense" category (see Chapter 11). But for most volunteers, these out-of-pocket costs *are* a financial consideration and good management requires the recognition and reporting of such agency resources.

Travel

This line item covers the cost of public outreach and recruitment. The director of volunteers and other program representatives will be making speeches and presentations throughout the community and such travel or public transportation should be reimbursed.

Travel also should accommodate trips to state and national meetings or conferences by volunteer program staff and participants.

Professional Development

Professional development includes funds for memberships in various professional societies (see Appendix B on volunteerism resources) and registration fees for workshops and conferences, both for the volunteer office staff and for *key volunteers*. This is one way that an organization can build loyalty among volunteers: demonstrate interest in *their* professional development, too. It is perfectly all right to ask that a volunteer make a commitment of time for all funds expended on his/her training—just as you would negotiate with a salaried staff member for a commitment in return for tuition reimbursement, etc. If the time commitment is not honored, then the person (salaried or volunteer) would be expected to pay back the money extended.

Volunteerism journal subscriptions and book purchases for an in-house library also fall into the category of professional development.

Volunteer Training

Training expenses may include fees to speakers, film rentals, books and handout materials, etc. to support volunteer training programs.

Other

Every program will have some sort of special need unique to its setting. The point to be made, however, is that volunteer offices often have "odd" requisitions. Who else may ask for 300 balloons?! The creative aspects of recruitment, motivation and recognition require supplies that set a tone or atmosphere different from the rest of the facility. So be prepared for the unexpected!

A Note on Allocating

While we have been discussing the allocation of a budget directly to the volunteer program, under the administration of the director of volunteers, it is also legitimate to provide for some of the expenses of volunteers within the budget of each unit that will involve volunteer workers. This allows for categorical accounting and may give you a more realistic understanding of the true costs of volunteer participation.

Finding the Funds

One of the purposes of budgeting is to recognize the total cost of running a program. However, nothing says that all budget items must be paid for out of organization monies. Quite a number of the items listed above can be covered by specific donations (both cash and in-kind) or by special fundraising events.

Remember that funds expended on volunteers are "leveraged" into more hours and types of service than the same amount of money could pay for in salaries. This multiplying factor can be a powerful argument to a corporate donor or to a foundation grants officer, who might well consider funding support of volunteers in your organization.

1 G. Neil Karn, "The No-Apologies Budget," *Voluntary Action Leadership,* Spring 1984, pp. 29–31.

VOLUNTEER PROGRAM BUDGET WORKSHEET

PERSONNEL

Director of Volunteers $ _____
    (Full-time or _____ hours per week)

Assistant Director of Volunteers   _____
    (Full-time or _____ hours per week)

Secretary   _____

Other assigned staff: _____
    _____

Benefits (estimated @ _____% of total salaries)   _____

(Estimate of cost of other staff time to train
and supervise volunteers: $_____)

                                Sub-total—Personnel: $ _____

OPERATIONAL COSTS

*Note that initial start-up costs are differentiated by an "S." Most of these items
are one-time expenditures, though several also involve additional purchases
each year as the volunteer program grows or to replenish inventory.*

Furniture and Equipment:

    Office furniture for the volunteer office,
    including desks, chairs, lamps, etc.   _____ S

    File cabinets   _____ S

    Typewriter(s)   _____ S

    Other equipment: _____   _____ S

Coat racks, storage cabinets, lounge furniture,
etc. for volunteers $_____ S

Bulletin boards and exhibit equipment   _____ S

Slide projector and screen   _____

                                    Sub-total—Furn./Equip.: $_____

Telephone:

Installation of instruments   _____ S

Monthly service charge × 12   _____

Toll calls/long distance × 12   _____

Reimbursement to volunteers for calls made
on agency's behalf   _____

                                    Sub-total—Telephone: _____

Supplies:

Office and maintenance supplies, estimated @
($_____ per person per year) ×
(salaried staff + FTE volunteer staff)   _____

                                    Sub-total—Supplies: _____

Printing and Reproduction:

Photocopying ($_____ /mo. × 12)   _____

Printing of volunteer office forms   _____ S

Printing (some typeset, some offset)
of recruitment materials   _____ S

Printing of recognition event certificates,
program book, etc. $_____

Production of periodic volunteer office
newsletter   _____

Printing of volunteer program manual/
handbook   _____ S

Other: _____   _____

*Note need to reprint inventory of some of the above
as an ongoing expense.*

                              Sub-total—Printing: $_____

Postage:

Regular correspondence, $_____ /mo. × 12   _____

Periodic mass mailings for recruitment   _____

Periodic bulk mailing of newsletter   _____

                              Sub-total—Postage: _____

Insurance:

(May be included in overall agency policy,
or a special rider, or a specific new policy.)   _____

                              Sub-total—Insurance: _____

Recognition:

(Depending on event, may include food costs,
entertainment, hall rental, gifts, pins, etc.)   _____

                              Sub-total—Recognition: _____

Enabling Funds:

    Reimbursement for volunteer mileage
    or transportation $ _____

    Reimbursement to volunteers for out-of-pocket
    expenses incurred while serving clients
    (ex.: purchase of art supplies,
    taking child to the zoo, etc.)   _____

    Purchase or loan of volunteer uniforms
    or special clothing   _____

    Other reimbursements: _____   _____

                        Sub-total—Enabling: $ _____

Travel:

    Volunteer office staff local and intermediate
    distance travel for recruitment outreach   _____

    Travel to state or national conferences
    (for salaried staff or designated volunteers)   _____

                        Sub-total—Travel: _____

Professional Development:

    Registration fees for seminars, conferences, etc.
    (for salaried staff or designated volunteers)   _____

    Journal subscriptions, books, etc.   _____

    Membership fees for professional associations   _____

                        Sub-total—Prof. Dev.:   _____

Volunteer Training:

    Reproduction of handout materials or
    purchase of books for volunteers $_____

    Slides and training materials   _____

    Film rental or purchase fees   _____

    Speaker fees   _____

        Sub-total—Training: $_____

    Other: _____

        Sub-total—Other: _____

        TOTAL COSTS: $_____

ALLOCATION OF ORGANIZATIONAL RESOURCES

    Staff time

    Space

    Maintenance services

    Access to organizational equipment and supplies

    In-kind volunteer benefits, such as meals

    Insurance coverage (possibly)

STAFFING THE VOLUNTEER PROGRAM

Decisions regarding the staffing of the volunteer program deserve careful consideration. How you go about designating or hiring the leadership of the program will be influenced by the goals you have for the utilization of volunteers. While it should be obvious that your staffing plan must fit the number and functions of volunteers you anticipate, it may not be obvious how to develop a "formula" to determine the right "fit."

Identifying a Leader

The vast majority of people who direct volunteer programs do not do so as a full-time job. Rather, they work part-time at volunteer management while actually primarily filling a different function in the organization; they have been asked to assume leadership of the volunteer program in addition to their other responsibilities. In many cases they were "annointed" into the leadership of volunteers; they did not seek the extra responsibility and felt they had little or no option when their administrator offered it to them. Additionally, they continue to view their original job description as their priority and try to "squeeze in" the volunteer program as a secondary set of tasks. In terms of career goals, most of these part-timers have no interest in pursuing the volunteer management field. They see themselves rather as "social workers," "park rangers," "occupational therapists," or "probation officers" and consider the volunteerism "piece" of their jobs as something they will escape when they move up.

Logically, someone who sees volunteer leadership as secondary (perhaps even as distracting) will rarely give the type of direction to the program that will make it achieve its true potential. So why "annoint" a reluctant director of volunteers?

The first step is to decide whether or not you are able (or willing) to create a new budget line for a volunteer program staff member. Since the dollar value of volunteer services far exceeds the actual funds expended (see Chapter 11), it may be worthwhile to wait in creating or expanding your volunteer component until funds can be found. A special fundraising event or a special grant request might create the first year's salary, especially if you plan to begin with a part-time staff member. At least this part-timer will devote *all* of his or her on-site time to the subject of volunteers. And the time will be devoted willingly and enthusiastically because it will be this person's primary job responsibility. The difference in possible achievement of goals because of this factor of *primary* responsibility cannot be overestimated and outweighs even the time limitations of a shorter work schedule.

If a new budget line is absolutely not possible, then you should begin by discovering who on staff might actually *want* to learn about volunteer management. Even if the interested staff member functions in a work area that seems tangential to what you plan for volunteers, the factor of free choice should weigh heavily in favor of giving that staff member the responsibility for volunteers.

When I conduct workshops for people who are part-time directors of volunteers in addition to carrying other agency job responsibilities, I always ask whether they tried to clarify the following important points at the time they accepted the volunteer-related tasks:

—What exactly does "part time" mean? how many hours of the day or week will I be allowed to devote to volunteer management?

—In what ways will my present workload be decreased in order to "make room" for my new volunteer program responsibilities?

—At what level of program growth will my part-time status be reviewed to determine whether more time is needed for volunteer management or if the agency is ready for a full-time director of volunteers (not necessarily me)?

—What other agency resources will be made available to me in support of the new volunteer program?

—Does my immediate supervisor understand and completely accept the fact that my previous work patterns will now have to change, especially in terms of decreasing my former output in my primary area of service?

In all too many cases, these questions are not raised by either the new leader of volunteers or the CEO. Because so many of these issues require decision-making authority, it would be helpful for the executive to consider these and other questions before selecting an existing staff member to take on the added responsibility of the volunteer program. Otherwise, volunteer management becomes nothing more than an addendum to an already busy schedule and, in fact, produces stress and tension among the staff as a whole.

It is probably just as pertinent to consider some of these issues even if a brand new employee will be hired to focus on leading the volunteer program as a sole responsibility, but on a part-time schedule. For example, at what point will you start thinking about increasing the number of work hours for the director of volunteers?

Whether you delegate volunteer management to an existing staff member or hire a new part-time employee, also assign specific responsibilities for supporting the volunteer program to other agency staff. This makes it clear that volunteers will be part of everyone's job because they are now part of the organization's delivery of services. For example, the public relations staff should help with recruitment, the bookkeeper with recordkeeping, and the typing pool with correspondence. It is up to you to distribute the work where it logically belongs and to specify the chain of command between the new head of the volunteer program and those other staff members' working on behalf of the volunteer program.

Even when you are ready and able to designate a full-time director of volunteers, other organizational personnel will continue to have support roles to play in assuring that the volunteers become part of the team.

- A corollary of being responsible for so many people is that no one else **coordinates** a staff with so many different schedules and so many different backgrounds. The director of volunteers must work with volunteers of all ages (possibly from children to senior citizens), of varying educational levels, and perhaps even with physical disabilities. Now add to this mixture the fact that volunteers select their own working schedules and you end up with something of a circus—with the director of volunteers as juggler! Some volunteers may work on a very exact, weekly schedule; others on an as-needed basis. Some come in every Monday and Wednesday morning, some all day Thursday, some every other Friday lunchtime, and some when the moon is full! The director of volunteers can never "call a staff meeting," yet is expected to organize the work of all these volunteers.

     Another dimension of this factor is that the director of volunteers ends up working in a "fishbowl" environment. Because volunteers arrive and depart at different times of the day, the director of volunteers is continually interrupted—legitimately—by the need to touch bases with the volunteer workers.

- Rarely does anyone else in an organization know how volunteers are recruited and managed. The director of volunteers is the **"in-house expert"** on volunteers and, in this capacity, acts as their advocate. This includes having to educate other staff about the ways to support volunteers and pointing out inappropriate requests for volunteer services. Volunteer management is such a new profession that the director of volunteers may feel isolated, while other staff may have colleagues in the same profession right there in the agency.

- The director of volunteers has a **triple constituency** while everyone else in the organization has only two. Everyone—including the director of volunteers and the volunteers themselves—must be concerned about the needs of the clients/consumers/patients. All activities must be weighed in terms of whether the best service will be provided to this public. Second, everyone must be supportive of the organization itself. This means that each person must uphold the policies of the agency and must work to achieve its mission. In fact, when an employee (or volunteer) can no longer support the organization's mission or policies, it is time to leave the job.

However, the director of volunteers has a third obligation: to represent the *volunteer perspective.* This point of view may sometimes be in conflict with the first two constituents and may, in practice, cause occasional tension between the director of volunteers and others in the organization. This is appropriate and the CEO should recognize that the director of volunteers is doing his/her job well when the volunteer perspective is expressed. It might help to recognize that the director of volunteers *facilitates* the involvement of volunteers . . . s/he does not "control" volunteers.

- The director of volunteers is the only person who has the **mandate to dream** about new projects without immediately having to limit such inspiration with the thought, "how will we pay for this?" Though volunteers are not free, they can test new ideas initially without much cash flow. This is a very special role for the volunteer office.

Given these things that make the director of volunteers different from other staff, you might consider how s/he can be of direct support to you as CEO. For example, are you involving the director of volunteers in your strategies for good public relations? Are you sharing long-range planning ideas with him or her so that volunteers can be integrated into planning from the very beginning? Are you utilizing the director of volunteers' across-the-board staff contacts to give you insight into the operations of the agency?

Qualifications for Being a Director of Volunteers

The field of volunteer administration is in its developmental stages. While you should seek someone to be your director of volunteers who has experience in the field, you may have to select someone with *potential* to learn the job. The following are some qualifications you might seek:

—Ability to articulate a positive point of view about volunteers: why they are important; what their potential might be in your setting; etc. This is a vital area—you don't want to hire someone with negative stereotypes about volunteers. How can s/he then help the rest of staff to work successfully with volunteers? Also, the self-fulfilling prophecy syndrome means that if the person is not positive about volunteers, s/he will never run a creative, energetic program.

—Vision—both of what volunteers can accomplish and of where your agency might go in the future.

—Strong management skills.

—Strong interpersonal skills. An effective director of volunteers has warmth and a degree of charisma. Potential volunteers are encouraged to join your organization through the image portrayed by the director of volunteers, their first contact with you. S/he must be able to convey friendliness and efficiency, and must also be able to get to know each recruit well enough to make appropriate assignments.

—Enthusiasm and energy. The director of volunteers creates an atmosphere for the volunteer program and it must be a lively one.

—Comfortable presentation style and public speaking ability. Remember that the demands of recruitment and training will put this person in the public eye and in front of groups often.

—Familiarity with community resources.

—Skill in task analysis, since work must be divided into manageable parts that can be assigned to volunteers giving a few hours at a time.

—Ability to handle/juggle details, especially the demands of scheduling and task delegation.

—Willingness to adapt good ideas from other settings to the special needs of your facility.

It is imperative that your director of volunteers be a good administrator. But it is *equally* imperative that s/he have the personality needed to be a *leader.* Since volunteers are not rewarded by a paycheck, the director of volunteers must have the ability to motivate people and to maintain high morale among volunteers (and salaried staff).

When you interview candidates for the job of director of volunteers, you might ask yourself whether you will feel comfortable in working with this applicant personally. As we have been discussing, the director of volunteers is in a position of genuine importance to you as the top executive. S/he should be an assistant to you in planning and implementing new projects. Also, s/he will be a representative of your agency in the community.

It is helpful to ask job applicants what volunteering they themselves have done in the past or are doing now. The way they answer this question—tone and enthusiasm as well as concrete details—should be a clue to their attitude about volunteerism. However, be careful not to fall into the trap of assuming that just because a person has done *volunteering,* that s/he is automatically able to *direct* a volunteer program. This line of reasoning is just as faulty as implying that any employee of an agency can also run that agency! Being a volunteer is useful background for understanding the value and potential of volunteers, but the skills of recruitment, supervision, recordkeeping, etc. are generally not gained by being a line volunteer handling specific client-related tasks.

On the other hand, if the person has been a volunteer administrative assistant in another volunteer program office, or has been an *officer* of an all-volunteer organization, or a coordinator of a fundraising event, etc., then you may be correct to assume those experiences would translate well into the management responsibilities of your volunteer program.

How to Find a Director of Volunteers

Increasingly, it is possible to find people with experience in volunteer administration. It is more important to seek someone who has demonstrated ability to mobilize volunteers in any setting, than to insist upon finding someone with a complete understanding of your type of facility. The setting can be learned more easily than the techniques of volunteer management. Also, you have lots of in-house resources to train the person about your setting. Who on staff can train the person in volunteerism?

If you accept the fact that volunteer administration is a generic profession, this opens the door to many recruitment possibilities. You might send a job opening announcement to any of the following resources (described at greater length in Appendix B), if they operate in your community:

   —the local Voluntary Action Center
   —the State Office of Voluntary Citizen Participation
   —the local "DOVIA" (Directors of Volunteers in Agencies) association
   —the regional officers of the Association for Volunteer Administration

Think about which facilities have large volunteer programs. If they are large enough to have several salaried staff members, there might be someone presently in an assistant position who is ready to move up into a full directorship. This might also be true of some administrative volunteers who have been, in essence, apprenticing as leaders of other volunteers. So it is worth sending a notice to such settings.

The skills of directing volunteers can be learned in non-agency environments, too. For example, anyone with background in organizing *successful* political campaigns (either for partisan candidates or for non-partisan issues) knows a great deal about volunteers. Former presidents of large, all-volunteer organizations also have experience in the nuances of organizing voluntary workers.

As time goes on, you may become aware of a growing number of people who have the credential of "CVA"—"Certified in Volunteer Administration." The CVA designation is awarded by the Association for Volunteer Administration, the field's national professional association. It is given after an applicant has completed a rather extensive certification process, including the development of a portfolio documenting performance-based competencies. The process includes peer review and has a built-in continuing education requirement. Applicants must have at least two year's experience in volunteer administration before they may begin the certification process.

If you interview someone with the CVA designation, you can be assured that s/he has demonstrated a commitment to volunteer management as a profession and a career. You can also be comfortable about the person's basic understanding of the role of a director of volunteers. Beyond that, you must determine for yourself whether the person fits into your facility and can handle the special demands of leading volunteers in your setting.

Many people fall into the field of volunteer administration unintentionally. (I did!) Because it is not yet possible to prepare for this profession through formal academic schooling, you will find that directors of volunteers come from a wide variety of backgrounds. On-the-job experience is what counts in most cases, though some applicants will also be able to document having attended single courses or continuing education workshops on various topics in volunteer management. In fact, if someone lists previous job experience in volunteerism, you should specifically ask what educational experiences s/he made use of. Has s/he ever attended a volunteerism conference locally, on the state level, or nationally? Does s/he subscribe to any of the journals in the field? These types of questions should quickly indicate whether the person has indeed connected her/himself to the "field" of volunteerism, beyond the daily tasks of the job.

Some people will apply for the job because they see it as a steppingstone into your type of setting. They are not necessarily interested in running a volunteer program, but rather want to do any job that will get them in the door. This motivation is not self-evidently bad, but it should be approached cautiously. Will this person devote him/herself to the needs of the volunteer program while s/he fills this position? Or will s/he look for the quickest way to move into another slot? The applicant must be open to the *possibility* that s/he will enjoy the position of director of volunteers enough to end up sticking with it and taking it to its maximum potential. You do not need a reluctant director of volunteers.

One reason why some people resist taking a job as director of volunteers is the mistaken impression that it is a field without a career "ladder." Because it is isolated in most settings from the other staff positions, there seems to be no clear way for a competent director of volunteers to move up. The real career mobility in volunteerism is to seek higher administrative responsibility (your job!). The director of volunteers is already in the perfect spot for learning a great deal about overall agency functioning. S/he will be involved in planning and implementation of a wide array of agency projects. If s/he is promoted into a Vice-Presidency or an Assistant Directorship, overall responsibility for the volunteer program can remain with that person—only s/he will now supervise the new director of volunteers. Directors of volunteers are actually in training to become CEOs—and when they reach that career point, they should be as supportive of the volunteer program staff as they always wanted their former bosses to be!

Secretarial Assistance

From the very beginning, a volunteer program needs the help of a secretary. This is as crucial to a part-time director as to a full-time one. If you have designated an existing employee as leader of volunteers, be sure to also designate consistent, available clerical support.

Recruitment campaigns, records on a growing corps of volunteers, preparation for such things as orientation or training sessions, recognition events, etc.—all demand a great deal of clerical activity. The program secretary also provides important office coverage while the director of volunteers is out in the community or busy elsewhere in the facility. Such coverage is vital because prospective applicants and active volunteers deserve to be able to make contact with someone who is knowledgeable about the volunteer program. Also, many secretaries actually supervise the work of volunteers assigned to tasks under the jurisdiction of the volunteer office.

One frustration often expressed by directors of volunteers is that their requests for a program secretary are met with the rather smug response: "why don't you get a volunteer to do it?" There is no doubt in the world that it would be possible to recruit a volunteer capable of handling the secretarial tasks of the volunteer office. The problem is one of schedule. One of the main purposes of a salary is to be able to "demand" a predetermined work schedule. If the director of volunteers has to rely on volunteers for necessary clerical work, then s/he may have to recruit as many as eight or ten volunteers to fill all the necessary hours of service. This creates a situation in which the services of volunteers "cost" the director of volunteers much supervision and coordination time—at the expense of other necessary work. A salaried secretary is a vital link in the program's operation. Volunteers can handle a great deal of the program's clerical tasks, but not those that need daily, timely attention with consistency and continuity.

In somewhat the same vein, executives tend to ask if it is possible to operate a volunteer program with a *volunteer* as the head. There is no

uniformly right answer to this question. It really depends upon whether or not you have a willing volunteer with both the capability and the schedule necessary to be the director of volunteers. Finding the capability is not the hard part—getting a long-term, multi-hour per week commitment is. If you are lucky enough to have someone available and willing to be a staff member at no salary, by all means accept his or her services. But recognize that you are not necessarily building for the future if you do not *budget* for an employee. It is better to create a staff position and indicate willingness to pay a salary, and then work with a volunteer for as long as that person can stay with you. In this way, if the volunteer leader has to resign, you are not caught completely unprepared to replace him or her. Volunteers able to give the necessary hours to head a volunteer program are few and far between. And if you end up recruiting, say, five volunteers to share the job—are *you* going to supervise and coordinate them?!

Many salaried directors of volunteers have indeed discovered that volunteers make excellent mid-level supervisors of other volunteers—sort of a team approach to running the office. Such administrative volunteers can be project coordinators for specific activities, orient groups of new volunteers, or follow-up on work being done by other volunteers off-site. This is one way that a director of volunteers is able to manage a growing program. It is a legitimate utilization of volunteers because it can offer flexible scheduling in reasonable chunks of time. However, even a program with several such administrative volunteers will eventually require a salaried assistant of volunteers, because the supervision demands of the administrative volunteers can also grow beyond what one employee can adequately give.

Graduate students majoring in some aspect of organizational management may be an excellent source of help in the early stages of a volunteer program or the piloting of a new volunteer project. If it is possible to develop a nine-month internship of two days per week and focus it entirely on volunteer program development, your organization may have found a cost-effective and reasonable way to get started. But do not forget that students are frequently inexperienced in the practical issues of management. Volunteer administration, as we have been discussing, is a rather sophisticated area that deserves the attention of a skilled manager.

Also, be certain to designate a supervisor who can genuinely help the student and who can carry on after the student leaves. In fact, it is important to plan ahead for the transition of leadership when the internship is over, because you do not want a gap in administration over the summer months or longer.

The danger of utilizing a graduate student is that the volunteer program may therefore be viewed as "low level," since the intern will hardly have real authority with which to make decisions or set standards. So your executive involvement in enforcing commitment to volunteers will be imperative.

If the volunteer program will be or is headed by a volunteer or a committee of volunteers, be alert to the possible ways conflict might develop between these leaders and the salaried staff—and do not unwittingly add to it yourself! The biggest problem is that the person may not be treated as a genuine administrator and will constantly be justifying her or his authority. Clearly, you will set the tone for the rest of the staff by the way you "model" acceptance of this volunteer.

Include the person, by name, on your department head memos. Invite the volunteer to staff meetings and give her or him time on the agenda as any other department head. Expect the same reports and other accountability from the unsalaried director of volunteers as you would from any other staff member. Supply the volunteer with an office, a telephone extension, and business cards paid for by the agency. All of these things demonstrate that the volunteer has been accepted by you as the leader of the volunteer program. Another important way to indicate that the volunteer is a part of staff is to show the program budget over which the volunteer department head has jurisdiction.

Other Staffing Needs

As mentioned in the rationale for a program secretary, the volunteer office has some special considerations in terms of coverage. Certainly every unit of the organization wants to be accessible to the public and therefore makes provisions for such things as telephone coverage when all staff are away from their desks. But for the volunteer program, this need is more than just for message taking. The hardest step in applying for a volunteer position is to make the initial telephone call. Therefore the attitude and tone of the person answering the phone on behalf of the volunteer program is critical. If the prospective volunteer hears disinterest or even discourtesy, the whole recruitment effort may be aborted. In fact, the agency representative should be saying things like: "we're so glad you called and I know that our director of volunteers will be delighted to call you back." This simply is not the way most staff "take messages" for each other!

As CEO, you can make certain that employees are trained to support the volunteer office in its relations with the public. Telephone switchboard operators, reception desk personnel and others with "frontline" public contact responsibilities should project a friendly and appreciative image to all prospective and active volunteers. In a small office, this requirement extends to all staff who routinely answer phones or greet visitors for one another. (This is a great example of behavior change that benefits everyone, not just volunteers!)

One other point is that the director of volunteers is *not* a substitute for volunteers. If a scheduled volunteer is absent for whatever reason, it is not appropriate to expect the director of volunteers to come to the unit and handle the volunteer's work for that day. This is, of course, no different from expectations we hold for employee supervisors. If an employee is not present, the work is generally held until the person returns; the supervisor does not step in to do it unless some emergency warrants it. Actually, since volunteers are deployed in the facility in various work areas, if a task assigned to an absent volunteer is critical, the most appropriate "substitute" would be a line worker in that unit—not the director of volunteers who is not part of that unit.

Volunteer Program Advisory Committee

Both for purposes of planning and evaluation, it might be helpful to develop an advisory committee for the volunteer program. Such a committee need not be large nor need it meet frequently. But it should be representative of management, line employees and volunteers themselves. When appropriate, recipients of service should also be included.

Because the director of volunteers must have a comprehensive overview of the whole organization, this committee can work to insure that all points of view are considered when new projects are begun. The committee therefore supports the director of volunteers by channelling information to the volunteer program and also by explaining program activities to others throughout the organization. This is an excellent way to prevent some of the possible tension between volunteers and salaried staff.

Enlarging the Apart from the job description and
Volunteer schedule of the leader of the volun-
Management Staff teer program, at some point you
will probably need to make decisions about when the program will require a full-time position, when to add one or more assistant directors of volunteers, and when to add one or more program secretaries.

It is difficult to give absolute guidelines for determining the right staffing pattern. However, the following criteria should be part of any discussion of personnel assessment:

> —Are volunteers going to be active evenings, weekends, or during hours beyond a "regular" work week? The answer to this question might immediately suggest the need for an evening volunteer supervisor, for example, or might help to determine the regular schedule of the full-time director of volunteers (11 a.m. to 7 p.m., for example, or Tuesday through Saturday).

> —What is the maximum number of employees that a supervisor is normally asked to supervise?

Some management books feel that no one should be expected to productively supervise more than five full-time people. Whatever your cut-off point in terms of employee management, apply it to the volunteer program.

First, what is the FTE ("full-time equivalent," as we discussed in the section on budgeting for supplies) of the volunteers working *directly* under the supervision of the director of volunteers? This might include volunteer positions such as clerical assistants, in-service trainers, volunteer office librarians, record-keepers, etc. The assessment of how many FTE volunteer staff are being supervised is especially pertinent if the volunteer office directly coordinates certain volunteer projects, such as an annual fundraising event or a daily meal delivery program.

Second, what is the FTE of the volunteers for whom the volunteer office is *indirectly* responsible (but still maintains records, handles recognition, etc.)?

How large would you allow your organization's salaried staff to become without adding to the number of employees in, say, the Personnel Office? The main point is to apply the same standards to the volunteer office and be sure that adequate staff is available to give the best management of the program. Keep in mind that one way you demonstrate your organization's commitment to volunteers is how you designate and then support the volunteer program's leadership.

1 Susan J. Ellis and Katherine H. Noyes, *No Excuses: The Team Approach to Volunteer Management,* Energize Books, 1981.

UNDERSTANDING THE VOLUNTEER/SALARIED STAFF RELATIONSHIP

It may be surprising to learn that the single most requested training topic in volunteer management is not how to recruit volunteers—rather, it is how to develop good volunteer/salaried staff relationships. Regardless of setting, age or size of program, everyone wants to know how to build an effective team between volunteers and employees. Why is this so hard? Is there something inevitable about tension between these two sets of workers?

One thing is certain. If the subject of volunteer/salaried staff relationships is ignored as a management issue, each employee (and volunteer) will develop his or her own way of interacting. Such diverse standards will indeed produce confusion if not out-right hostility. The main purpose of this chapter, therefore, is to emphasize the need for *the involvement of top administration in setting the tone and policy for effective integration of volunteers into the organization.* This cannot be left in the hands of the director of volunteers. S/he does not have the *authority* to make rules for the whole organization or to enforce such rules. As the nonsalaried personnel of the organization, volunteers deserve direct attention from the executive level.

To assess whether your agency has planned sufficiently for good volunteer/salaried staff relationships, consider the following questions:

—What happens (in terms of actual procedures) when a volunteer makes a mistake or does something wrong?

—If a dispute develops between a volunteer and an employee, is the employee always presumed to be right? Is the employee presumed to have more rights?

—Are there clearly defined channels for volunteers to make suggestions, voice criticisms, etc.?

—How many members of the salaried staff have ever had formal training (not just on-the-job experience) in how to supervise volunteers?

—Has any member of staff recently refused to work with volunteers (this means refusing to develop a job description for possible volunteer assistance—not turning down a specific applicant who was not appropriate)? Why? Did anyone question that staff member on his/her refusal?

—Has any employee ever been evaluated on his/her level of competence in supervising volunteers?

—When was the last time an employee was given any tangible recognition for working successfully with volunteers?

—Is it common practice to refer to the "professional" staff versus the "volunteers"?

—Do all labor contracts (if you have one or more employee unions) include clarification of the role of volunteers in the agency and, especially, their role in time of a possible strike?

—How many volunteers have left the agency in the past year due to dissatisfaction with their acceptance level in the organization?

If you answered these questions honestly (and no one will ever know, so go ahead!), you might find yourself saying "I'm not really sure." *That's* "benign neglect." If all these questions were reversed and asked about salaried staff, you'd feel responsible as a manager to know the answers. Volunteers tend to be invisible workers.

These questions hint at some of the key volunteer/salaried staff relationship areas requiring policy formation and top administrative involvement.

One situation crops up so frequently that it is often not even perceived as a problem at all: the
premise that an employee has the
**Danger Signs:
Refusal to Accept
Volunteers**
choice of whether or not to work with volunteers. In many ways,
this is the crux of the entire problem and so deserves scrutiny.

In most organizations, the director of volunteers recruits
volunteers and, after screening applicants, matching them to the
most appropriate jobs, and orienting them, assigns them to the
day-to-day supervision of salaried staff. Some volunteers do work
under the direct supervision of the volunteer office, but the majority are "deployed" throughout the organization in a decentralized
approach to volunteer management. The premise is that line staff
are the ones most knowledgeable about the tasks to be done and
therefore should work directly with volunteers in accomplishing
those tasks.

If you are going to institute a volunteer program or
strengthen the one you already have, you must deal with the question: do we, as an organization, believe *qualified* volunteers are
vital enough to integrate them everywhere? Please note the word
"qualified." In every instance, this book is advocating the appropriate placement of volunteers who either were recruited for special skills or were given training by the agency to fill necessary
positions.

Some of the resistance to working with volunteers comes
from stereotypes about what volunteers are like. Employees
should never be asked to work with uncommitted, unqualified, or
unpleasant people—whether unsalaried or salaried! But if we start
with the supposition that the volunteer program will be managed
well and that all volunteers will be recruited to match the requirements of available assignments, then prejudices about volunteers
should be dispelled.

As long as salaried staff are given the choice or act as though
they have the choice of accepting volunteers as co-workers, top
administration is sending mixed messages about volunteers. The
implication is that working with volunteers is in some way "additional" to the primary work to be done. Despite the fact that the
organization has established a "volunteer program" and allocated
resources to it, utilization of volunteers is viewed as an option that
any individual staff member is free to accept or reject. When no
negative reaction follows from an employee's decision not to

work with volunteers and, further, when the employee who does work with volunteers receives no positive reinforcement, the only logical conclusion is: *it does not matter to administration.* Volunteers are "nice" and maybe even "helpful," but they are certainly not *essential.*

Think what would happen if, using a hospital as an example, a nurse unilaterally decided s/he would not work with the physical therapists. Whenever the PTs come around, s/he politely refuses to work cooperatively. Such behavior sounds so absurd it is even hard to take the example seriously. Yet, in hospital after hospital around the country, the Volunteer Services Department has had to accept rejection from nurses and other medical staff who simply—with no reasons given or required—opt not to "take" a volunteer.

In most organizations right now, the director of volunteers is placed in the position of going around to the salaried staff and asking: "do you want a volunteer?" The tone is one of, can we do each other a favor? How ridiculous. If the organization has seen fit to establish and fund a volunteer component, then it is a part of the agency. All salaried staff must collaborate with that unit in exactly the same way they are expected to work with the physical therapists, the typing pool, the maintenance staff, or the public relations department.

The director of volunteers must be held accountable to find and prepare the best possible volunteers. If s/he cannot do this, it is grounds for dismissal. But if the director of volunteers is indeed fulfilling this responsibility, then no other staff member has the right to judge the volunteer program negatively—and therefore must cooperate. If an employee is uncomfortable with volunteers, the proper administrative response should be to *offer training,* not to permit him or her to avoid this aspect of the job.

Ironically, some directors of volunteers have contributed to the perpetuation of this cycle of "acceptance of rejection." They do not confront the resistant employee on the grounds that they prefer not placing volunteers into a negative supervisory situation. So, out of reasonable concern for the morale and motivation of the volunteers, the director protectively ignores the staff member who refuses to work with volunteers. While this may be proper management in the case of a particular volunteer ready to work immediately, it is poor long-range planning. The director of volunteers must identify resistant staff members and—with the help of the chief executive—change their behavior.

Even if the salaried staff understand **What Causes**
the value of volunteer involvement **Tension**
to the agency and its clients, in day-
to-day operations the interface
between the two sets of workers can be difficult. Both the perspective of the employee and the volunteer must be understood in
order to analyze what causes tension between volunteers and salaried staff. Specifically, it is necessary to identify:

> —the perceived threats posed by volunteers to salaried
> staff; and,

> —the reasons volunteers may be resistant to supervision by
> salaried staff.

Because this is first and foremost a human relations situation, it is helpful to remember that the dynamics involved do not
always relate to real issues but reflect fears, misunderstanding, and
prejudice—on both sides. So in order to prevent or solve interrelationship problems, it is necessary to consider the *possible* factors
involved.

Here are just some of the real or **Threats to the**
imagined threats volunteers pose to **Salaried Staff**
employees. This list is not meant to
imply that every staff member har-
bors these fears, but to show that there is a wide range of possible
reactions to the offer of volunteer assistance. Please note that
some of these issues are not mythical. If the staff senses that
administration does not recognize some of the possible problems
volunteers create, they will be reluctant to tell you their genuine
reactions to the idea of volunteers—instead, they will undercut
the program by refusing to be given a volunteer or by providing
insufficient supervision to volunteers already on board.

> —Volunteers will take salaried jobs . . . maybe my job. *Here
> is a good example of just because you're paranoid, it
> does not mean someone is not out to get you! Is it really
> strange that in today's economy, staff are fearful for
> their jobs? And have you ever discussed volunteers as
> budget "savers" rather than as budget "extenders"?*

—Volunteers will do a bad job and I'll be left with the blame, or the responsibility to "clean up."

—Volunteers will do a great job and I'll look less effective. *(Return to threat #1 . . . will a great volunteer replace me? In fact, what do you think is most threatening? A volunteer who fails or one who succeeds? Because of uncertainty about the* true agenda *behind the involvement of volunteers, the most effective volunteer programs are frequently the ones with the biggest staff acceptance problems.)*

—Volunteers are spies. (To whom are they related? To whom do they talk after work? Are they watching the way I perform?) *The reality is that volunteers do indeed see the work being done—and not being done. If an employee is insecure about his or her performance, the thought of a volunteer uncovering weakness is scary.*

—Volunteers are amateurs. They do not know much and I'll have to train them from scratch, which takes a lot of time.

—Volunteers are highly trained and they do not want to be oriented to do it our (my) way. They can't be controlled.

—Volunteers are different from me. They are (select any that apply) younger, older, less educated, more educated, a different race or religion, from a different social or economic class, more or less knowledgeable about this community, etc.

—Volunteers gossip. They do not understand confidentiality.

—If these volunteers were really good workers, they'd all have paying jobs. (You mean a lot of them already do? Then how come they're also volunteering?)

—I do not know how to break my work into smaller tasks that can be delegated to a volunteer. I am also not sure that the time it would take me to do this would be won back in any savings by having the volunteer help me. Besides, I'd really rather do it myself so I can be certain it will be done right.

—I never learned about volunteer management in my formal education, so I'm not sure how to work with volunteers. But, because I take pride in being a "professional," how can I admit that I don't know how to work with volunteers?

—Volunteers want to spend too much time socializing with me.

—We have so little work space. I don't have the room to work with a volunteer.

—Volunteers are not dependable.

—You can't criticize a volunteer, so how can you make sure the work is done right?

—The client may like the volunteer better than me.

—All the things I can think of for a volunteer to do are the fun parts of my job. I don't want to give those up.

—I am jealous (though I'd never show it) that volunteers get all those thank-you's, special luncheons, and balloons. And they also get to choose their schedules and their work assignments. They even get to say "no" once in a while.

—My supervisor doesn't understand that working with volunteers takes some of my time.

—When I accepted this job, no one ever told me I was supposed to work with volunteers.

—There are no rewards for working well with volunteers.

—Why should I work with a volunteer? Volunteers
"belong" to the director of volunteers and why should I
do him/her the favor of supervising a volunteer?

—I am so new at my job that it is hard for me to explain
parts of it to a volunteer.

—Volunteers only see a small part of the picture because
they come in irregularly. Therefore their opinions and
suggestions are not worth as much as mine because I
understand the whole situation.

—If we act on all these new ideas, things will change
around here.

—Do I have to say thank you all the time—even if I don't
mean it?

—Volunteers interrupt my day/week.

In examining the range of these statements, it is obvious
that even the best salaried staff members may be concerned about
some of these issues. And in all honesty, their concern may be
appropriate, especially if the organization has never clarified its
policy about volunteers.

There are indeed practical issues involved in accommodat-
ing volunteers which salaried staff should be encouraged to identify and discuss. These include such things as: volunteers *do*
require staff time; volunteers *do* have more options for saying no;
some volunteers *are* on board in order to learn new skills and
therefore need extra attention in training.

Another factor is the diversity of your volunteer corps.
Some volunteers will be recruited as highly-trained specialists,

while others may come to your organization as trainees or to fill generalist roles such as friendly visiting. Unfortunately, this diversity sometimes results in all volunteers being judged by the lowest common denominator. For example, because one unit utilizes high school students as volunteers, staff in another unit may be skeptical about the qualifications of volunteers who may be referred to them—they simply have trouble visualizing more skilled voluntary assistance.

Special Cases

Certain employees may have more justification than others for questioning the value to them of working with volunteers. Brand new staff members, for example, are so busy learning the ropes of their job that they really cannot yet delegate parts of it to someone else.

Some jobs or professions are not "people-oriented" in that they involve limited contact with the public and the type of person entering them may prefer it that way. These jobs range from library cataloguer to zoo keeper to chef. At the very least, such staff members are inexperienced in supervising other people and may resent having this responsibility foisted on them "after the fact" of accepting a job description without mention of volunteers.

Finally there is the growing number of paraprofessional positions. Paraprofessionals are usually low on the "pecking order" of an organization anyway. They are directly threatened by the influx of volunteers because many of the things assigned to volunteers are related to the assistant work performed by paraprofessionals—and so job security is an honest issue. Negative attitudes by paraprofessionals about volunteers are compounded by the fact that often it is the paraprofessional who is assigned to supervise the volunteers—and very few paraprofessionals have the training, the time, or even the skill to do this adequately. If you have a paraprofessional level of staff, be alert to the possibility of misunderstanding of roles between them and some volunteers.

Volunteer Resistance

It takes two to tango. Though the majority of problems between volunteers and employees stem from employee actions, in all fairness, volunteers also contribute to the hostilities. Their real or imagined reasons for resistance may include:

—I am more qualified than the salaried staff, so why should I let them boss me around?

—I am here to help out and the staff should be grateful. What's all this about requirements and commitment?

—The employees are different from me. They are (select any that apply) younger, older, less educated, more educated, a different race or religion, from a different social or economic class, more or less knowledgeable about this community, etc.

—I am not sure what the salaried staff really does. Am I doing their job? What are they doing while I do their job?

—Why should the salaried staff get paid while I don't (especially if I'm doing their job)?

—I am always told what to do, but am never asked to participate in planning the work.

—My suggestions are not listened to. People here seem unwilling to make changes.

—The salaried staff gets/takes credit for my good ideas.

—No one says thank you.

—Volunteers always seem to get the "idiot work" around here.

—No one ever gives me feedback on my work. I wish I'd know how useful my efforts are or how I might improve my work.

—I am given jobs to do without being told their context, so I never really understand how my efforts fit into the activities of the organization.

—I always have to search for a place to do my work and there is nowhere to store my work from week to week.

—My grandmother founded this organization and these new staff members are not doing what she would have wanted.

—I should be treated as special because I am related to one of this group's (select one:) board members, donors, top executives, legislators.

—Salaried staff are always given the benefit of the doubt in any dispute. They are seen as "right" just because they are on the payroll.

—Whenever I come in, the employees are always at lunch, on a break, or in a meeting. Don't they ever do any work?

—I am given very little training or even good instructions. I am not sure who to ask if I have a question, especially if my supervisor is at lunch, on a break, or in a meeting.

—The staff is moody and often does not say hello, goodbye or thank you.

—I do not know who runs this place. A lot of people come and go from the front office, but I've never been told who they are. They rarely greet me in the hall.

—I don't like the label "volunteer." Can't I have a title?

—I'm just a volunteer.

Of course, you may be heading an organization in which there are many more volunteers than salaried staff. In such circumstances, the salaried staff realize that volunteers are vital, but some volunteers may misinterpret their numerical strength and feel superior to the salaried staff. This manifests itself in volunteers "giving orders" to the staff or resisting when staff delegates work to volunteers.

Diagnosis   The litany of possible attitudes just presented is intended to demonstrate how wide a range of causes there might be for tension between employees and volunteers. View both lists as a sort of "menu" from which to select the specific issues that might be at work in each tense situation. The dynamics of a particular confrontation will be unique to the individuals involved. And keep in mind that *veteran volunteers* can display the same reaction to "newcomer" volunteers as the salaried staff do! As CEO, much will depend upon your skill in diagnosing what is really going on beneath the surface.

Research what the actual circumstances are and therefore which attitudes stem from facts or myths. If a person has had a negative experience, it is unrealistic to expect him or her to be completely open to a second try. For example, if a salaried staff member worked hard to train a new volunteer and then that volunteer left the agency unexpectedly, it is obvious that the staff member will be wary of the commitment of future volunteers.

Sometimes it is helpful to consider why certain salaried staff members or volunteers are exceptionally receptive to teamwork with each other. Knowing the reasons for *good* relationships can indicate approaches to take to change negative relationships. Possible factors that would make for favorable support of volunteer involvement include:

—Personal history with volunteerism in another setting—if that past experience was positive.

—Respect for the work of the director of volunteers.

—Direct experience with excellent volunteers or salaried staff (as opposed to direct experience with mediocre volunteers).

—Praise from an executive for innovative work done with/ by volunteers.

In the next chapter we'll examine some of the other considerations that make for positive reinforcement of volunteer/salaried staff teamwork.

STRATEGIES TO CREATE TEAMWORK

As chief executive, you have a vital role to play in laying the groundwork for productive teamwork between salaried and volunteer staff. There are several concrete things you can do to establish policy and standards for your organization.

Job Descriptions: Employees

First, you can make certain that all job descriptions for employees include a statement about volunteers. In some cases, the job description will indicate that a staff member will have responsibility for supervising volunteers personally. In other cases, job descriptions may simply note that this is an organization in which volunteers are active and therefore all employees will have to interact positively with them. For department heads or middle managers, the job description might clarify that volunteers will be active in each component of the organization and that the department head will be expected to develop appropriate job descriptions, delegate work to volunteers, and help supervisees to work effectively with volunteers.

If all employee job descriptions contain references to interaction with volunteers, then the job application process should also attempt to uncover a candidate's background in volunteerism. For example, include a question on the written application form that asks about the candidate's personal volunteer experience (you will undoubtedly discover many valuable things about the person's interests and other job-related qualifications from this question, as well as gain a sense of this person's understanding of the concept of volunteerism). In the interview, you should ask whether the candidate has ever supervised volunteers and in what context. It is helpful to ascertain whether the applicant has ever received formal training in volunteer management, either in a classroom setting (unlikely) or on the job in another organization.

Job Descriptions: Volunteers

In the volunteer management profession, there is universal agreement that volunteers deserve written job descriptions. Such descriptions clarify roles and differentiate what volunteers do from what the salaried staff do. Writing down an assignment is not a paperwork exercise. It provides a tool that will be used in recruiting the right volunteer, in determining the necessary training for the job, in holding the staff accountable for supervising the volunteer, and for evaluating the work performed. Therefore it is also the basis for recognizing the achievements of a volunteer, or for initiating the process of termination.

The volunteer job description allows the director of volunteers to conduct a meaningful interview with an applicant. It demonstrates that your organization is not simply looking for people to "help out," but is hoping for productive work to be accomplished. On this basis, it is possible to screen out prospective volunteers who do not fulfill the job description's qualifications—without creating any bad will for turning away someone who offers assistance. You set standards from the beginning.

The salaried staff member who will be working with the volunteer directly must be involved in writing the job description. This presupposes two requirements:

1) that the staff member's own work is efficiently organized so that someone else can assist with it; and
2) that the person is skilled in task analysis and can divide the work into manageable pieces to be delegated.

The latter is why the director of volunteers has an important role in helping the supervisor to define a reasonable, appropriate volunteer assignment. Having to write something down is a good way to insure that there is indeed a meaningful job to be done.

As CEO, you should stress the value of written volunteer job descriptions. See to it that time is taken to articulate these correctly and that they are reviewed as often as necessary to remain current. This action alone may alleviate many of the problems between volunteers and salaried staff. When people know what is expected of them, they are happier and more productive.

By the way, think about showing volunteers the job descriptions of the salaried staff, too. This makes the circle of understanding complete and documents that volunteers fulfill roles that are different from, but parallel to, those of the employees.

Once you have stated the expectation that salaried staff will work with volunteers, make certain that all present employees understand **Training**
how to work with volunteers. Keep in mind that almost no one receives training in volunteer management as part of formal schooling and so there should be no shame in admitting uncertainty about successful techniques of volunteer supervision. If the staff are in any profession dealing in human services, be alert to the fact that they might resist the notion that their in-house interpersonal skills need some sharpening! Social work begins at home, and many people who provide wonderful service to "clients" are unable to develop teamwork with those they label (often incorrectly) as "nonprofessionals."

The only way to be certain that staff will approach volunteer supervision consistently and in accordance with your policies is to provide training. The key is to demonstrate the importance of the subject by allocating time to it. Remember, very few staff will have learned the techniques of volunteer management in their formal education and so people may be surprised that you are devoting several hours to this subject.

Staff training must deal with attitudes as well as with skill development. For example, uncovering the stereotypes that employees have about volunteers is the first step toward new understanding. One interesting way to approach the whole subject is to give employees the chance to talk about the volunteering that *they* are doing outside of the job (or something they have done in the past as a volunteer). This sets up the concept of the Golden Rule—comparing how the employee likes to be treated when s/he is a volunteer with how s/he treats volunteers in the agency. It breaks down the barriers of "us" and "them."

Directly confronting some of the fears and threats about volunteers is also healthy. Discussion of the individual "pay-offs" for developing teamwork with volunteers and a review of the agency's benefits from involving volunteers deserve some attention.

Sometimes there is the problem of vocabulary. It is common to refer to salaried staff as the "professionals." The dictionary does define "professional" as "one who earns a salary for one's work." This is the distinction between "professional" and "amateur" athletes, for example. But in most organizations, the word "professional" is used to connote someone who has special *training.* Staff must be helped to see that not all volunteers are untrained. There are many volunteers who are as equally "professional" as any member of the salaried staff, but who are willing to offer their services as volunteers to the organization. It is insulting and therefore tension-producing to differentiate paid and unpaid staff with the word "professional."

By the way, once you have trained your current staff in volunteer supervision skills, do not overlook the possible training needs of new employees you may bring on board later. Be sure to include some time in the volunteer office in the orientation schedule of new staff members, so that the director of volunteers can brief the newcomer about the way in which volunteers are integrated into your organization's services. Assess whether the new person requires more in-depth training, especially since you cannot assume s/he learned about working with volunteers at a previous job.

Pilot Testing

As already mentioned in the chapter on planning, it is always a good idea to start small, by pilot testing new assignment areas for volunteers. If salaried staff feel overwhelmed by a sudden influx of a cadre of volunteers, how can an effective partnership develop? Allow time for the integration of volunteers to take place and for employees to gain confidence in working collaboratively with volunteers.

Supervision

Salaried staff in general do not have to learn all the techniques of how to develop and run a volunteer program. That is the responsibility of the director of volunteers. But to accomplish specific jobs, the staff should feel comfortable in supervising and collaborating with volunteers as co-workers. All the principles of good supervision of employees operate with volunteers, too. However, there are some special considerations to supervising volunteers. These include:

- The need to create a positive working "atmosphere." Because volunteers come and go during the course of a day or week, they encounter the work environment of a particular period. If the work site tone is harried and has-sled, it will affect volunteers' approach to their work, too. If some volunteers are on duty at lunch time and there-fore always see the staff on "break," they will sense a different atmosphere than those who are scheduled at a peak client visitation time. Enthusiasm and energy are infectious and really help volunteers to feel motivated. (Creating a good atmosphere for volunteers is one of those elements of volunteer management that rub off beautifully on the salaried staff. Everyone benefits from a positive tone in the working environment.)

- Many volunteer assignments involve work to be done outside of the agency's offices. This type of field work includes such independent responsibilities as home visits to clients, solicitation calls on potential donors, leader-ship of group activities (clubs, sports teams, trips). It is quite possible for a volunteer to serve the organization entirely separated from the work site of the supervisor or staff liaison. This physical separation requires special consideration for defining lines of communication and accountability.

- Volunteers need accessibility to a supervisor or someone designated to answer questions. If an employee has a question and discovers her/his supervisor has gone out to a meeting, the question can wait until the next day. But a volunteer may only be in once a week. In that circum-stance, having no one who can move the work forward can amount to a waste of a work day. It is not sufficient to have another staff member hand the volunteer a pile of work to do (though this is light years ahead of having the volunteer arrive only to discover no one remembered s/he was coming in and no work was left at all!). Concern must be shown for supporting the volunteer's accomplishment of the task.

- The volunteer's commitment of time should be respected. If there is no work to be done in the person's assignment area on a particular day, then the volunteer should, in all courtesy, be contacted and told of the problem. S/he can be given the option of revising her/his schedule for the week or of coming in anyway to do some other task. But it should not be assumed that all volunteers will do "anything" just to help out.

  As alluded to above, nothing is more undercutting of the volunteer's commitment than to arrive at the job and discover that no work has been prepared—in fact, to realize that the salaried staff had forgotten the volunteer was even due in. Watching the employee rush around to "pull something together" for the volunteer to do is hardly conducive to the feeling of really being needed.

- There is something in the volunteer world that I have always called "instant accountability." This refers to the reality that, in the supervision of employees, there is a margin for error that does not exist with the supervision of volunteers. If a supervisor is moody, uncommunicative, nasty, or leaves no work to be done in his/her absence, the salaried worker will not like it, but will tolerate it—or perhaps will "wait out" the mood until a better day. But the volunteer who is treated discourteously or is left with nothing to do is quite likely never to return to the organization again. This is not to imply that volunteers are thin-skinned. But if one gives one's time to a facility and then is treated poorly, why should one return? It is a form of masochism or martyrdom to wish to repeat a bad experience under those circumstances.

  It might be a measure of a supervisor's skill to realize that every time a volunteer *returns* to an agency it is a compliment to what occurred on the previous visit.

- Volunteers have freedom of choice beyond what employees are usually given. Employees must complete a wide variety of mandated tasks, even some that are tedious or somewhat unpleasant. A volunteer is free to say no to an assignment, without jeopardizing his/her right to remain a volunteer. This does not mean that a volunteer can randomly select which parts of a task to do and which to ignore. But it does mean that the person can, within reason, select a particular assignment on which to work.

- There is a degree of "socializing" that is part of volunteering. This can get out of hand, at which point it becomes a reasonable complaint of the employees. But, within bounds, it is fair for a volunteer to want to have some personal interaction during his or her scheduled work time. So long as this does not interfere with productivity, it means that the supervisor might show an interest in the volunteer's activities since last seeing him or her.

- Recognition, especially in the form of saying thank you, is important to supervising volunteers. In some ways this amounts to an "exit line" in which a person is acknowledged for his/her efforts that day and is encouraged to return. Volunteers do not always see the way their work fits into the larger picture. By next week, the project handled this week may seem forgotten—unless the supervisor notes how the effort enabled the entire workload to be completed. Again, it would be nice to say thank you more often to employees, too.

Two important concepts to keep in mind when supervising volunteers are *courtesy* and *self-fulfilling prophecy.* So many interpersonal relationships can be handled smoothly with politeness and friendliness. This is important for any human interaction, but with volunteers the need to be courteous is even more vital. Similarly, when one expects the best, one often gets the best. If one has a low level of expectation about volunteers, volunteers will act accordingly—largely because they will end up being poorly recruited, trained and supervised.

Salaried staff often want to know if they may criticize a volunteer. The answer is—of course. In fact, it is a form of compliment to give a person suggestions for improving work done; it implies that the supervisor has confidence that the volunteer has the capability and will to do a better job. And then the volunteer knows the work is important enough to be reviewed and done to the best of everyone's ability. Empty thank you's without enthusiasm leave volunteers with the uncomfortable suspicion that their work will be tossed out after they leave. It is better to deal directly with improving a volunteer's work. After all, when people give their time freely, it is in the hope that their effort will produce results—not to waste their time doing something wrong or ineffectively.

Liaison Supervision by the Director of Volunteers

The director of volunteers maintains an ongoing relationship with volunteers placed throughout the organization and monitors the progress of volunteer assignments. The immediate staff supervisor is responsible for day-to-day supervision, specific to the job to be done. Should any problem arise, that supervisor is the first line of communication and accountability. However, the director of volunteers can be helpful to both the employee and the volunteer by being a third party to differences of opinion.

If the volunteer wishes to change assignments, it would be up to the director of volunteers to weigh the request and act upon it. Similarly, if the staff member wishes the volunteer transferred or terminated, the director of volunteers must be involved. Ideally, the interrelationship is cooperative and open.

Collaboration with Volunteers

Not all volunteers work "under" salaried staff supervision. There are a wide variety of assignments that utilize volunteers as independent specialists, as consultants, or as project leaders. These job descriptions genuinely imply partnership between volunteers and salaried staff, on an equal footing. In fact, in some cases the volunteer's position (and expertise) may place him or her above the salaried staff member in rank. (See Chapter 8 for a discussion of board roles.)

The principles of good volunteer "supervision" create effective teamwork, too. Clear job descriptions, respect for the volunteer's time and contributions, plus a willingness to be honest about the value of the work produced, encourage successful collaboration. One special need in these types of assignments is clarification of how the volunteer will keep the organization informed about her or his activities. Specify a *two-way* reporting process and timetable.

Enforcement and Recognition

Once you have seen to it that all staff receive the necessary training in how to work with volunteers, the next step is to enforce the process by evaluating salaried staff on whether they are carrying out this job function appropriately. Employees should receive feedback on their effectiveness with volunteers as a part of any annual or periodic performance review. This implies further that special effort and achievement with volunteer assistance will receive special recognition (a raise, promotion, or at least a comment)—and that poor teamwork will also carry negative sanctions. Only when good behavior is reinforced and bad behavior carries consequences do an organization's standards carry weight. Unless you are willing to act in this manner, you are only giving lip service to "support" of volunteers—and the salaried staff will each decide unilaterally whether or not to cooperate with volunteers. Without the risk of administrative disapproval, it is easy to opt for not working with volunteers.

To be fair, enforcement is a two-way street. Volunteers should also be held to high standards and there should be consequences if productivity is low or work is not done properly. If some volunteers show poor attendance or resist instruction, they should be informed of the organization's dissatisfaction. This is as important as providing recognition for volunteers who do well. In fact, it makes annual recognition events more meaningful if everyone knows that mediocre volunteers were weeded out. The salaried staff will be more likely to accept evaluation of their ability to work successfully with volunteers if they know that the same assessment will be made of volunteers.

Pay-Offs to Individual Employees

Naturally you do not want employees to team with volunteers just because there is punishment for not doing so. Rather, you hope salaried

staff see the benefits of volunteers to the organization and themselves. But it is important to remember that the benefits to the
agency for involving volunteers are not at all the same as the "pay-
offs" to an *individual* employee who takes the time to supervise
volunteers well. For example, just because the *agency* might
receive good public relations from informed community volunteers, it does not follow that a particular salaried staff member
feels rewarded directly for the effort of working well with
volunteers.

What are some of the benefits or "pay-offs" to an *individual* employee? Consider the following:

—When a staff member supervises volunteers well, s/he
demonstrates to administration (you!) that s/he has managerial ability.

—Supervising volunteers is, indeed, on-the-job training for
supervising employees.

—Volunteers bring a freshness of approach that can help the
employee to see his/her work in a new way.

—Volunteers share the staff member's interests and can
therefore reduce isolation and provide support in a way
other staff often cannot.

—Since volunteers provide the luxury of trying new service
approaches without the agency having to seek funding
first, volunteers can test a new idea and prove its merit. If
the idea to be demonstrated is the employee's, s/he has
the chance to show her/his value to the organization.

—Volunteers can lessen the work load by handling a variety
of helpful tasks.

—Volunteers can free the employee to do things s/he is spe-
cially trained for or likes.

—Both of the above can reduce employee tension and prevent burnout.

—Qualified volunteers can handle aspects of the work for which the employee may actually not be trained or best suited.

—Volunteers can stimulate creativity by adding new ideas and responding to staff innovations.

—Because volunteers may have a range of different life experiences, working together can provide personal enrichment for the staff.

Settling Disputes

Just because someone is a member of the salaried staff does not necessarily make his or her point of view "right" or more worthy of consideration if it differs from that of a volunteer. Intellectually this point might be acceptable but, in practice, management actions can imply that employees get the primary benefit of the doubt.

It is true that full-time employees, or even part-time employees with weekly schedules, see a broader picture than a volunteer with limited time on-site can. Also, demonstrating loyalty to a staff member with seniority is understandable. But every situation must be weighed in terms of its particular details, so as to insure that volunteers are not discriminated against.

How does such discrimination occur? One example is the case of a large metropolitan hospital in which the director of volunteers received a memorandum from an administrative assistant in another department concerning access to the photocopying machine. The memo asked the director of volunteers to instruct all volunteers whose assignments included photocopying to stop their work whenever a salaried staff member came to the copying room and to turn the machine over to the employee. In other words, the administrative assistant felt that employees had "first rights" to the copying machine. What are the underlying assumptions of this memo?

First, the memo implies that the time of the employees is "clearly" more valuable than that of the volunteers (after all, they have the time to volunteer, so they can wait around, right?). Second, the memo shows misunderstanding of what volunteers are doing in the photocopying room—they are (surprise!) making photocopies. And these copies are being made for departments/employees who need them as part of the hospital workload. So first come, first served is a reasonable rule in the photocopy room, no matter what the hourly rate of the person making the copies.

Actually, the full-time employee has more options as to when to return to the copying room. The volunteer, with a limited daily schedule, needs to complete as much work as possible in the allotted time. So asking the volunteer to wait around while the employee does copying turns out to be more wasteful of productivity than may be realized.

The most notable fact about this memo is that it was sent at all, in the complacent certainty that the salaried staff had the right to dictate the use of organizational resources. It expressed the opinion that volunteers should do "whatever it is they do" only when it does not "interfere" with the really important activities of the employees.

The way to begin to deal with such attitudes is to recognize them when they surface. As chief executive, you have the chance on a daily basis to reaffirm that volunteers are legitimate workers with equal access to resources. If the volunteers' assignments are appropriately planned, their need for workspace, supervision, and even copying machines can be accommodated with a minimum of stress.

If individual disputes occur between a member of the salaried staff and a volunteer, these should be handled in the same manner as any interpersonal problem. The two people should first be encouraged to work out their differences together. It should *not* be acceptable for the employee to unilaterally decide: "I just can't work with this volunteer; ask him/her to leave." If necessary, the employee's immediate supervisor can mediate the problem, possibly also calling in the director of volunteers for assistance.

The volunteer's point of view deserves to be heard and to be evaluated on its own merit. Of course, if there are facts that the volunteer is unaware of because of his/her limited schedule or other considerations, these should be explained. But again the bottom line is that a salaried staff member cannot rely on being seen as "right" *a priori* on the basis of being on the payroll.

If volunteers are indeed in the wrong, the staff should feel that standards will be maintained and that such nonproductive or counter-productive workers will be asked to leave. It is probably necessary to mention that volunteers should also not be protected against criticism or even "firing" simply out of gratitude for their voluntary service.

Reassignment of a volunteer to a new unit or to a new staff supervisor may be an appropriate way of solving a particular interpersonal problem. But reassignment should not be expected "on demand" of an employee. This is another version of giving staff all the power with no accountability for their skills in supervision.

Unions

If labor unions are active in your facility, the question of volunteers will come up sooner or later in contract negotiations. There are just as many examples of peaceable relations between union employees and volunteers as there are examples of tension. The way to insure peace is to *plan in advance.*

Bring up the subject of volunteers well before labor relations become problematic. There are really only two issues about volunteers that concern union leaders: will volunteers be used to replace employee positions, reduce overtime pay, or prevent new salaried positions from being created; and what will be the role of volunteers during a possible employee strike?

The latter is simpler to handle than the former. The basic rule about utilization of volunteers in a strike is to treat volunteers as individuals capable of making their own decisions. If volunteers wish to continue with their ongoing assignments during a strike, they should be permitted to do so as a matter of personal choice. However, administration might assure union members that no *new* volunteers will be recruited or mobilized during a strike—nor will volunteers already on board be re-assigned to cover work that strikers normally handle. The bottom line for unions is to receive assurance that volunteers will not be utilized as *strike breakers* to provide the agency with a work force capable of holding off the strikers for a long period of time.

It is legitimate to agree to thoughtful utilization of volunteers during a strike as much for protection of the volunteers as out of fairness to employees. But on the other hand, do not agree to refuse to allow volunteers admittance to the facility if a strike is on—this violates each volunteer's right to choose his or her own position.

The question of "taking jobs" is much more difficult to clarify because almost every organization utilizes volunteers as a way to stretch the budget beyond what available money would otherwise be able to "buy" through employees. While each administrator must honestly deal with the suspicion that volunteers will be used as a way to *cut* a budget, at the same time it is justifiable to firmly assert the position that management has the right to locate and utilize whatever resources will allow the organization to meet its goals and serve its clientele.

Here is an area in which volunteer job descriptions are invaluable. Administration should be able to document that it is the intent of the organization to recruit and assign volunteers to positions that are substantially *different from* the roles filled by employees. This does not mean that all volunteer positions have to be "subservient" to employees. It simply means that the slots to be filled by salaried staff are the ones shown in the budget and that the job descriptions written for volunteers would not be filled by employees under any circumstances.

It is probably useful to clarify with union representatives whether or not volunteers will be utilized as a temporary measure if an employee leaves a job, until a salaried replacement is found.

To prevent future tension, it might be helpful to encourage union representation on any advisory committee or evaluation team supporting the volunteer office. But beware of giving the union the power to OK or veto volunteer job descriptions. If your policy of not duplicating staff roles is accepted, the day-to-day implementation of this should not be given to the union for oversight.

Budget Cutting   Perhaps this is a good point to discuss legitimate concerns about budget cutting, since salaried staff are so often wary of new volunteer projects because of questions of job security. Many organizations are faced with an impossible choice: the need to reduce spending while maintaining or even increasing services. Some groups may wish to expand services but recognize that additional funding will be hard to find. This is the type of situation in which it is very appealing to conclude that "we'll do it all with volunteers." The fallacy of this simplistic approach has already been discussed. Volunteers may be "free" in the sense of not requiring a great deal of cash outlay, but they are very expensive in terms of recruitment, training, coordination, and supervision time.

It is next to impossible to "fill a gap" left by a full-time employee with only one qualified and available volunteer—it would require an intricate schedule of several volunteers each giving a certain number of hours per week and each bringing the organization a different set of qualifications. Take all the concerns of "job sharing" and multiply them several fold!

One other mistake is to assume that somehow it will be easier to find volunteers to handle the low-level, clerical jobs of the agency. Under this assumption, when the budget diminishes, all the "professional" staff are retained but the secretaries are let go. The irony is that the organization can survive more reasonably if the public relations staff is cut back or if there are three fewer caseworkers than by losing someone to answer the telephone during all working hours! Equally ironically, it is easier these days to find volunteers willing to handle the more challenging assignments of, say, writing the organizational newsletter or helping a family to learn budgeting than to get a full shift of volunteers to do typing or envelope stuffing.

The best way to handle the real problem of a reduced budget is to reassess the job descriptions of the *entire* staff. This means doing a task analysis of the way things really work in the organization, not just what was put on paper in the distant past. Scrutinize the various tasks that each employee is doing and identify the following sorts of things:

—what is someone doing once a week or periodically, rather than daily or on an inflexible schedule?

—what is someone doing that really does not require his or her specialized training? (For example, a lot of time is spent in making follow-up telephone calls, composing letters, etc. that may take someone away from direct service to clients.)

—what is someone doing that might be done more effectively by someone else with special training in that skill?

Once you have identified these specific tasks, you are ready to re-align all the job descriptions. *Re-write the salaried staff positions* so that these contain all the things that require daily attention, special training, etc. Add the similar critical responsibilities that had been assigned to the "cut" staff members, so that the remaining employees are primarily now assigned to the most important, daily functions. Remove the other periodic or less technical responsibilities—which then become the basis for legitimate *volunteer* job descriptions. You will be asking volunteers to handle work that can be done on a once-a-week basis or that makes use of special talents for which the volunteers have been recruited.

This approach to the unfortunate need to trim the budget is therefore good management of both salaried and volunteer staff. You will be paying for the best utilization of your employees and will attract volunteers in support of your organization. It is also hard for unions to be as negative about this approach, though careful negotiation is probably in order.

Teamwork Prognosis   When analyzed in the way we have just being doing, the factors that affect teamwork between volunteers and salaried staff are not mysterious. In many ways they are the same factors involved in the interrelationships of members of the salaried staff. The major difference is that people expect to define paid work roles, but too often overlook the same need for clarification of volunteer roles. Assumptions fill the gap when there are no established policies—assumptions that may well be wrong.

While some initial tension between volunteers and salaried staff may be understandable, there are equally important benefits to each for establishing a sense of partnership. By paying attention to the issues just described, the outlook is very positive for real integration of employees and volunteers.

Finally, it is worth re-emphasizing that the last two chapters have contained concepts basic to good management—regardless of whether or not the workers to be managed are volunteers or employees. The most effective ways to support volunteers are also the best ways to work with salaried staff—not the other way around. The organization that creates a positive working atmosphere for its volunteers usually also benefits from the high morale and productivity of its salaried staff.

SPECIAL CATEGORIES OF VOLUNTEERS

One of the most exciting things about involving volunteers is that the potential for tapping the resources of your community is limitless. When you develop a volunteer program, you give its leader the mandate to recruit whatever assistance can effectively meet your organization's needs. This opens the door to all sorts of creative utilization of people and cooperation with other organizations. Avoid defining "volunteers" too narrowly. Seek out the widest range of community resources through your volunteer program office.

We have already recognized that volunteers come with every possible type of background and characteristics. In this chapter, we'll examine some special categories of volunteers that are legitimately recruited and administered through your director of volunteers, but which require some top executive involvement in decision making and policy setting.

Students

As CEO, you define the categories of workers in your organization. If your agency is a placement site for college or graduate students completing "internships," there may be some debate over whether or not these students should be coordinated by the volunteer program office. Coordination of student interns is an administrative issue that is separate from the question of who should *supervise* such students once they are working in the organization. Do not allow the waters to be muddied by either the academic institution or various "professionals" in your agency. The volunteer office has a clear and supportive role to play in the effectiveness of internships . . . and here is why:

- From the point of view of payroll, student interns are just as much "volunteers" as any other volunteer. Interns work in the agency for benefits other than financial reward. Academic credit cannot be negotiated at the store for a loaf of bread.

- There are indeed differences between student interns and other volunteers, but these are considerations related mainly to what the interns will be asked to do and who will supervise them. Often a school will ask for special training experiences to make the internships more valuable. In terms of management, these considerations are not very different from the need to match any volunteer to the best assignment or to accommodate such factors as physical disability. The volunteer office, therefore, can keep the list of all available internship job descriptions and do *initial screening* of all applicants. Then it should be up to the actual staff supervisor to make the final decision on *acceptance* of the intern (just as with any volunteer who would be assigned to a unit).

- By utilizing the volunteer office to centralize all internship applications, you save staff time in contact with the various colleges and you make sure that any internship applicant is told of *all* available openings. If individual staff supervisors make the first contact, they will only be aware of what is available in their one particular unit and will not offer the prospective intern the full range of assignment options for the entire organization. Similarly, if a student is not right for one unit, only the volunteer office has the overview necessary to see if there is another possible placement that would be more appropriate.

- If you do not utilize the volunteer office, where will records be kept on student interns? Is anyone keeping such records at all now? As executive, don't you want to know how much staff time is being spent on interns, how many students you have assisted, or what the performance level of interns has been? If for no other reason, it may be necessary to document the work of interns to meet insurance requirements (since, as with all volunteers, there are accident and liability considerations for interns).

- Many student interns contribute far more hours to the agency than the minimum required by the school. Is this extra time not "volunteering" in its purest sense? Also, a percentage of students will want to remain active with the agency after the official end of their internships. Will you then expect them to "transfer" to the volunteer office—or will they remain undocumented (and, actually, unauthorized) in an unclassified state? In a workshop I taught recently, a participant admitted that she knew of at least three students who had kept right on with their work for over a year after their school ties had ended, but no one reported it until she asked why the young people were still around. Some of their co-workers in the unit were not even aware that the official internship had ended. Parenthetically, is this the best way to help students with their education? Maybe these students were ready to move on to more challenging assignments in another part of the organization, but no one was "responsible" for making this offer to them.

- Every newcomer to the agency deserves an orientation. If interns by-pass the volunteer office and go directly to their line supervisors, they will not get an overview of the entire organization. The volunteer program is already set up to offer orientation and students should have access to it. Training for the specific task to be done will be given by the supervisor, as is appropriate.

- From a public relations standpoint, if you do not centralize the coordination of internships in the volunteer office, you are expecting the various schools and colleges to track down as many staff supervisors as necessary to place what may be several students. Working through the volunteer office would allow the faculty to make one contact a semester, referring all the student internship candidates at one time. Similarly, requests for end-of-placement evaluations can be channelled through the volunteer office (one call for the school), so that the director of volunteers can monitor whether all forms have been submitted as required. Copies of such evaluations can then be kept in the volunteer office with the student intern's other records, so that future references can be made easily.

- A number of years ago, the only student internships were those in medicine, nursing, teaching and social work, and the type of placement and professional expertise of the supervisor required were clearly defined. Today, there are "internships" in a wide variety of subjects ranging from geography to communications. These newer internships are not always so definitive in requiring a certain fixed set of experiences. Whether the internship is of the "traditional" kind or the more unstructured, experiential learning kind, the volunteer office is your agency's best vehicle for screening applicants and determining suitable assignments.

- Finally, without the involvement of the volunteer office, it is unlikely that students will receive formal recognition of their accomplishments during their internships. Only you and the volunteer office can represent the entire agency in expressing appreciation.

Apart from internships in which the student is committed to a specific schedule for a duration of time, there is also the question of student "observers." You should have some policy defining your organization's point of view on such observation, largely because it is time-consuming for the staff without necessarily contributing anything to service. Once again, the most logical administrative umbrella for student observers is the volunteer office. The director of volunteers can make the arrangements with the school, schedule appropriate visits, keep records of the activity, and perhaps even recruit some of the students as ongoing volunteers!

Finally, a growing number of high schools and even some junior high schools have instituted limited forms of student internships in community agencies. Because these interns are teenagers, it is usually less controversial to suggest that they are also "volunteers." In reality, the same arguments form the rationale for allowing the volunteer program office to administer internships at any level.

Community-conscious businesses have long participated in charitable efforts. In recent years, however, corporate philanthropic efforts

Corporate Volunteerism

have received increased attention. The phrase "corporate volunteerism" is comparatively new and refers to the involvement of a company's employees as volunteers in community organizations. Of course employed people have always been active as volunteers, but "corporate volunteerism" implies that the company itself, as the employer, takes a direct role in encouraging the public service involvement of its employees. It has also come to be an umbrella term for some of the in-kind services businesses provide at no cost to nonprofit organizations.

From the purview of this book, what is important about corporate volunteerism is that you and your director of volunteers may have to work cooperatively in approaching corporations for assistance. You may be requesting a financial contribution from a company, but may also want to recruit its employees (or retirees) as volunteers. It is important to present a unified management team, rather than find your organization has contacted a corporation from several angles at once—looking as though the left hand does not know what the right hand is doing. Also, it is becoming more and more usual for a business to respond to a request for money by offering a "package" of funds, in-kind services, and employee volunteers. As executive, will you be able to utilize such a package effectively without planning together with the director of volunteers?

There is no reason to make corporate volunteers into a special category all by themselves, even if the volunteers are "release time" employees of the corporation. If they are going to fill existing volunteer job descriptions, they should be integrated into your organization's corps of volunteer workers, just as would volunteers from any source. In most cases the company employees will actually be volunteering on their own time, so there is even less reason to differentiate them from other volunteers. The only exception might be technical assistance volunteers, which we will discuss in a moment.

When the director of volunteers seeks volunteer assistance for your organization, s/he often uncovers ways to get needed services at no cost or at highly reduced cost. Such development of in-kind contributions is a part of the role of the director of volunteers which you should cultivate and support. It is one of the sometimes hidden aspects of the job that can be misinterpreted as overstepping boundaries (since the director of volunteers is generally not authorized to "fundraise"). Recognize that, in this context, the department of volunteers is really the "department of community resources." This provides a much more realistic concept of the possible forms of donated services a good director of volunteers will turn up: in-kind, barter, exchanges, collaborations, loans, and volunteers.

Technical Assistance Volunteers

In a number of communities, special projects are functioning that recruit highly skilled volunteers willing to provide technical assistance consultation on a short-term basis to any agency with need for such help. This is often called a "skillsbank" and allows its volunteers the chance to donate their expertise to a wide variety of community agencies. Some corporations have established their own skillsbanks, registering interested employees and then informing local agencies of the types of skills obtainable.

Some of the skills offered are concrete, such as carpentry, art talent, or computer programming. For such skillsbank volunteers it is not difficult to create suitable "assignments" and evaluate success. The bookshelves are built, the brochure designed, the records entered. However, many of the skills available through skillsbanks are less tangible, ranging from expertise in strategic planning to personnel policy development. This type of technical assistance implies that an organization is willing to open up its management process to consultation from the volunteer—and it means that the top administrators will be directly involved.

Working with a volunteer consultant is no different from working with a paid consultant in terms of the potential benefits from the shared expertise. Many of the techniques for maximizing paid consulting time also apply to getting the most from a volunteer expert: proper identification of the needs to be addressed; homework on your part to offer the consultant useful background materials; good agenda planning; follow-up of recommendations. But technical assistance from a volunteer does require some special attention to show that you value the volunteer's time and opinions as though you were indeed paying for these in cash.

Regardless of whether the technical assistance is provided to management or to the custodians, the director of volunteers has the same responsibilities in the process as with any other volunteer. The short-term technical assistance role is simply one more type of volunteer assignment.

Group Volunteering

Many types of volunteer assignments bring together groups of volunteers to accomplish the work. Sometimes the volunteers are individuals who happen to be scheduled for the same shift, but sometimes an already-established community group agrees to provide several of its members to volunteer in your facility together. Whether the source is a church, synagogue, school, corporation, or civic organization, keep in mind that one of the reasons the source is supporting your volunteer project is to develop a sense of identity and unity among its own group members. This may or may not interfere with your desire to generate loyalty to your organization in people who contribute to you as volunteers.

All group volunteering is coordinated through the volunteer program office, but the point to remember as CEO is that your organization has formed a collaboration with another organization. Be sure that lines of authority and communication are defined, and that group volunteers receive the same orientation and training as would any other volunteer. Clarify possible issues such as insurance coverage, especially if organized groups participate in one-time special events, such as large fundraisers.

Informal Volunteers

In the course of a program year, you may find that your organization benefits from the "help" of individuals who informally give a few hours of their time in some way. Most often such volunteers are family members or friends of the staff or of current volunteers. And they frequently surface during major fundraising or public events, when your organization needs lots of support work such as carrying boxes, staffing booths, and cleaning up. Such informal contributions are wonderful. The only caveat is to assess the situation and make sure that, if someone is really serving for many hours on an annual basis, you are not simply permitting loose management just because the person is not on the payroll. If someone can be identified as volunteering, perhaps the volunteer program office should enroll him or her more formally. This permits better utilization of the volunteer, inclusion in the thank you's that follow an event, coverage by your insurance, and the most accurate documentation of community contributions to your organization.

Court-Referred Volunteers

A growing trend in criminal justice today is alternative sentencing, in which an offender is given the option of completing a set number of hours of community service work in lieu of a fine or spending time in prison. There are many models for such alternative sentencing programs, but all are looking for organizations willing to offer placements to program participants. If you agree to accept court-referred volunteers, you will probably need to set related policy.

Some of the policy areas to determine are:

—Whether you wish to place any limits on the nature of the offense or on the minimum amount of hours in the sentence (for example, it may not be cost-effective for you to orient and place someone who has less than 20 hours of community service work to do, unless you have a number of short-term projects waiting to be tackled).

—How much you need to know of the person's court record before placing him or her. Who in your organization will be told of the person's sentence and for what reasons.

—How you will handle possible infringements of the place-ment agreement, should they occur. For example, after how many absences will the probation officer or other court contact be notified?

—Whether court-referred workers will be assigned to the same jobs as other volunteers and how this might affect the overall volunteer program.

Once again, use the volunteer office as the conduit for these court-referred workers. They are nonsalaried, temporary person-nel who require screening, orienting, etc., just as all other volun-teers do. This is also a way to be sure the proper legal records are kept to verify the time served.

Interestingly, data on existing alternative sentencing pro-grams indicate that a large percentage of people referred by courts to community service work continue to be active as volunteers well after their mandatory time is over. This is a positive side-effect for both the person and the organization.

Another special group of volunteers needing top administrative clarifi-cation relates to the concept of "self-help." It may be important to

Residents or Clients as Volunteers

your delivery of service to encourage those who are generally seen as recipients to, in turn, become givers by participating in the program as volunteers. Some examples of this type of volunteer-ing include:

—When retirement center residents take an active role in visiting, feeding and helping other residents who are ill enough to be in the infirmary.

—When patients in a long-term mental health facility help in tending the gardens and grounds.

—When students do a major clean-up project within their school building.

—When residents in a home for the severely disabled form an active program committee that plans year-round spe-cial events.

—When seniors in a nutrition center help to set the tables before and clean up after their lunch.

The common denominator of all these examples is that there is a very fine line between what might be reasonably "expected" from program participants versus what is some type of "extra" service that warrants the label of "volunteer." Every organization must come to its own definition of what makes a resident or client a volunteer—and how this group of volunteers differs from "outside" volunteers. In practice, this includes such questions as: will the residents who volunteered be invited to the annual volunteer recognition event?

Some of the types of resident or patient volunteering are really an attempt to foster *participation* in the facility's program so that the experience is more home-like or therapeutic. Other types of client involvement encourage "ownership" of the activity and reduce the feeling that the person is receiving "charity." Self-respect is thereby maintained while getting necessary work done.

The key variable in all this is *choice*. Each person must participate completely voluntarily and should have as wide an array of options for particular assignments as possible. It is choice that places such activity within the realm of volunteering.

Some organizations have run into difficulty implementing a client-as-volunteer program because of protests from those outside the facility. The major point raised by such protestors is that the clients are being utilized as unpaid labor. Several court cases have successfully enjoined agencies from continuing certain types of programs using patients or residents as workers, unless a minimum wage is offered. In most of these cases, the evidence revolved around whether the clients truly had the choice to say no to the work activity.

If you wish to implement a self-help volunteer project, be sure to clarify the issues involved and to utilize the director of volunteers in establishing some structure. It would be highly appropriate to ask the clients themselves for input from the very beginning.

Specially-Funded Programs

There are a number of federal, state and local government programs that pay participants a stipend or even a full salary to work in selected community agencies. Such programs often are focused on a particular target population that is difficult to employ, such as teenagers, senior citizens, the disabled, or non-English speakers. The program models range from ones in which the recipient agency pays a percentage of the worker's salary to ones in which the organization has no financial obligation at all.

As CEO, you will need to make a determination as to which workers are to be considered employees and which volunteers. One reasonable approach would be to place any worker receiving financial payment under your personnel office, while placing non-remunerated workers under the volunteer office.

For bookkeeping purposes, this division on the basis of money works quite well, but there are other considerations to insure smooth organizational functioning. If the special salaried workers are part-time and/or not clearly skilled, perhaps the director of volunteers needs to be part of the assignment-making process regardless of who maintains chief responsibility for these workers. Once again, who else maintains an ongoing list of the available short-term work in the agency or is prepared to conduct an orientation at any time?

In addition, it is important to make sure that a temporary influx of stipended workers does not displace loyal volunteers. This does not mean that a new source of help should be turned down. It simply suggests that present volunteers should be considered in your planning process and should be approached for suggestions as to what they would most prefer doing, should they be "replaced" by paid newcomers.

Conclusion

If the director of volunteers is seen consistently as heading the organization's "Nonsalaried Personnel Department," the interrelationship of all of the above categories with all other volunteers becomes apparent. Once you have made the various executive decisions necessary to authorize the director of volunteers to coordinate the full range of volunteers as just described, your organization will benefit from all available community resources on an ongoing basis.

EXECUTIVE-LEVEL VOLUNTEERS

This book is focused primarily on direct service or "in-house" volunteers. But most organizations also benefit from the services of another group of volunteers: those who make or affect policy, or who raise funds. All nonprofit organizations have a volunteer board of directors. Many organizations also have auxiliaries, a different category of volunteer activity. Finally, a wide variety of advisory councils involve community volunteers. For some units of government, such advisory councils may even be mandated by law as an opportunity for citizen participation.

In almost all cases, the top executive is the connecting link between such volunteers and the rest of the organization. In this chapter, we'll examine how the principles relating to in-house volunteers apply equally to these special types of volunteers.

THE BOARD

A great deal has already been written for the CEO on working with boards of directors. Though the fact that boards of directors of nonprofit organizations are comprised of volunteers is acknowledged without argument, in practice the voluntary nature of boards is frequently overlooked. So it is pertinent here to discuss how the successful utilization of in-house volunteers is applicable to making boards of directors more effective.

Recruitment and Job Descriptions

For example, recruitment of new board members can be done following the model of how to recruit direct service volunteers. Targeting potential sources of board members on the basis of special skills needed or type of representation sought is one way to find the right people. Similarly, having written job descriptions to show candidates will clarify what your organization expects of each board member. For board officers, additional job descriptions are needed to describe the requirements of each leadership position. By using job descriptions at the start of a board member's term, you are able to hold people to their commitments—whether this involves attendance at board meetings, follow-up activities during a given month, or a financial contribution.

By the way, there is a misconception that an organization's by-laws already provide job descriptions for board volunteers. The by-laws define *functions* and division of responsibility, but do not specify the practical, operational aspects of filling a board position. Also, the by-laws deal with functions that are continuous and timeless. Job descriptions, which should be updated regularly, apportion tasks necessary at any given point in time.

Be honest in writing board member job descriptions. Do not underestimate the time commitment involved in serving on the board. Remember to mention the work expected of board members in-between regular board meetings, including preparing in advance for the meetings and serving on sub-committees.

If you hope for—or expect—a financial contribution from every board member: say so. It is reasonable to ask the board to demonstrate their support of the organization with a donation. By openly stating this expectation, you can later solicit money from board volunteers more comfortably.

Developing Effective Working Relationships

Orientation and training are as important for board members as for any other volunteers. Regardless of the expertise for which the board member was recruited, no one is able to walk into a new situation and start being productive without learning the details of that particular situation. It is never insulting to offer board members the opportunity to learn about your organization—and someone who resents such a session is probably an inappropriate recruit.

In your role as chief executive, you will be providing leadership to the board in ways that are very different from "supervising" in-house volunteers. One major difference is that the board is in charge; they have the final legal responsibility for the way your organization operates. Authority and power rests with them (even if some boards rarely exercise their power), including the right to hire and fire the chief executive. Even more sobering is the realization that the board of directors can legally make the decision to close the entire agency. Some boards make that decision by default, by not raising sufficient funds. But some boards make the active choice to end services, which may reflect the happy fact that those services may no longer be needed.

In order to make the best decisions for the agency, board members need your executive direction and advice, particularly in identifying the most pressing issues for the organization at any given time. Your most effective tool is persuasion—explaining to and convincing the board of your point of view. You also need to provide resources with which board volunteers can accomplish tasks, explain how their work integrates with the rest of the agency's timetables, and also monitor that board work is getting done. All this requires setting a tone of harmony and energy— motivating board volunteers to give their utmost to the organization.

Periodically, it is nice to provide some recognition to board members for their hard work on behalf of the agency. It is too easy to become wrapped up in the problems of today and overlook the achievements of the past year. Again, because board members are volunteers, doing something to say thank you is always valid.

In some smaller (and even larger) organizations, board members become active in the daily work of providing services. In fact, the traditional way nonprofit organizations grow is that board members do *everything* in the beginning—from making policy to cleaning the office. Later, when funds are raised, a small corps of salaried staff takes over the operational side of the agency and the board redefines its role to goal and policy setting. This transition is not always accomplished without pain. It is hard for board members to relinquish control over activities they handled before the staff came on board. To some board volunteers, the hands-on work is more interesting than the policy decision-making and they prefer doing "practical" things.

On one level, it is healthy for board members to have some first-hand exposure to the work of the organization. It is questionable how a board can make decisions without some "reality test-ing" of the possible effect of certain actions. Also, needs assess-ment cannot be done objectively if all the data is funnelled through the CEO's perspective only.

You and the board must establish the boundary line between yourselves in your own way, based on the needs of the organization at this point in its history and on the personalities/skills of the individuals involved. But it is important for you to recognize that roles must be *defined.* If a board member volun-teers on-site on a regular schedule, then s/he should be "super-vised" in much the same way any line volunteer would be. The dual demands of authority figure and direct worker should be sep-arated as much as possible.

Sub-Committees of the Board

Depending on the type of sub-committees your board has desig-nated, certain members of the sala-ried staff may be assigned as "liaison" staff to support the committees' work. This interface requires clarification of roles. For example, will the staff member be a voting member of the committee, or serve ex-officio? For that matter, is the staff member expected to participate fully in discussions, or merely be present to act as a resource when requested?

The matter of who takes the minutes (both for the full board meeting and for sub-committees) deserves examination. Because this task seems clerical, it is common for volunteers to delegate this to salaried staff. Unfortunately, this serves to assign the "power of the pen" to the staff. Minutes present facts but also subjective interpretation of what was discussed. The written record of a meeting continues to influence the organization. Vol-unteers should retain the responsibility for reporting their own deliberations and decisions.

There are no clearly right or wrong ways to develop work-ing relationships between the board and the staff. The variables of each organization must be considered. But the volunteer manage-ment principle of *defining* how the teamwork will operate is something that only you, as executive, can employ.

The Board Treasurer

The role of volunteer board trea-surer is a special one and deserves attention here. The board of direc-tors is responsible for the financial stewardship of the organization. The board member for whom this is a primary focus is the treasurer.

What this means in practice will change as your organization grows. If you have limited staff, the treasurer may actually keep the books. Or you may have this responsibility as part of your job description as executive director. Later, the agency may hire a bookkeeper. Eventually, there may be an entire accounting or finance department, with the previously-volunteer position of treasurer evolving into a salaried position within a board of trustees.

Until the organization has a full staff of employees working on finances, the board treasurer should be directly involved in monitoring the finances. This means physically coming into the agency regularly to provide oversight to the bookkeeper, co-signing checks (at least those above a board-agreed-upon amount), and generally assuring internal control. Even when there is a staff to handle such daily transactions, the treasurer still provides oversight. As long as the position is held by a volunteer, the treasurer should *present* the organization's financial statements to the board and be able to answer any questions related to them. The financial statements should explain in financial terms what you present in the narrative of your executive director's report.

The treasurer has the right—indeed the obligation—to *ask questions*. S/he watches what the organization is spending money on and thereby provides control for the board.

How the Director of Volunteers Can Help

The director of volunteers can be a real asset to you in building up the board. Ironically, too few CEOs think of their director of volunteers in this context—yet who in the organization knows more about the demands of working with volunteers? Specifically, the director of volunteers can help you in the following ways:

- Because the director of volunteers is out in the community, s/he can be of assistance to the board nominating committee in suggesting possible candidates to join the board. Also, the director of volunteers can identify active, committed line volunteers who might be valuable board recruits because of their first-hand understanding of how the organization functions.

- The director of volunteers has lots of experience in writing volunteer job descriptions. Why not put this skill to work for the board?

- When designing an orientation for new board members, why start from scratch? The director of volunteers has already developed a curriculum, handouts, and perhaps even audio-visual aids that s/he uses to orient in-house volunteers. Most of this material will be equally applicable to board members and you can add whatever other information you need.

- Board members should be included in any agency volunteer recognition event. To this end, the volunteer office could assist you in keeping records of board member activities, so that each board volunteer can be recognized for his/her special contributions. Any person who volunteers for the organization is a valuable resource—whether that voluntary service is given directly to your consumers or indirectly through policy making.

- Finally, the work of the board may be accomplished through sub-committees. These might be composed entirely of board members, or of a mixture of board members and non-board volunteers. The director of volunteers can certainly recruit non-board volunteers to join such committees and can train salaried staff to provide liaison support to these committees. Such "support" is another version of good staff/volunteer relationships.

There is no reason to keep board members and other organizational volunteers apart, especially by creating a hierarchy whereby board volunteers are treated much more respectfully than any in-house volunteer ever is. Both groups are community members and, in their own ways, have clout.

How the Board Can Help the Volunteer Program

You might consider suggesting to the board that they create a sub-committee to support the volunteer program. This might be called the

"Volunteer Resources Committee." Its role would be to help in establishing policy for in-house volunteers, to assist the director of volunteers in recruiting volunteers, and to take an active role in evaluating the program.

AUXILIARIES

There is no single model for how an auxiliary should support an organization. Quite diverse types of settings utilize auxiliaries. The list includes: hospitals, long-term care institutions, libraries, cultural arts groups, and law enforcement agencies. Sometimes the group goes by a name such as "The Friends of ___" and may provide in-house volunteer work in the sponsoring organization's offices. But most often an auxiliary's major purpose is to raise money.

Historically, auxiliaries were responsible for the funding of most of the institutions we hold dear. Also historically, auxiliaries were female organizations —frequently the wives of the staff or of the board members. In some cases, the auxilians raised the money and turned it over to the decision-makers of the sponsor group. In other cases, the auxilians participated in determining how the money would be spent. These two approaches still exist today. In some organizations, the president of the auxiliary has a seat on the board of directors.

For the purposes of this book, what is important about auxiliaries is to recognize their volunteer nature and to analyze whether you, as executive, have created the best working environment. You should assess:

1. Is the interrelationship of the auxiliary and your agency clearly defined? Is the auxiliary autonomous or do you, as sponsor, have some formal decision-making role to play in its governance?

2. Who are the members of the auxiliary? What are the criteria for joining and are new members recruited with these criteria in mind? Does the auxiliary perpetuate exclusionary practices such as limiting membership only to women, to people able to pay membership dues, etc.? If so, are these discriminatory practices justifiable?

3. Is the auxiliary still strong or is it a remnant of its old self from years ago, with members aging fast and no longer able to give or generate financial contributions comparable to those in the past?

4. Is there an actual or *implied* hierarchy in which the auxiliary has more status than the in-house volunteers?

5. What is the relationship between the auxiliary officers and the director of volunteers? Is there a direct line of authority (in what direction)? Why or why not?

6. Does the auxiliary president expect and receive direct communication with you as CEO? Why or why not?

7. Do you receive regular reports from the auxiliary on all aspects of its operation, including membership statistics and financial statements?

8. If the auxiliary is not self-incorporated, what is the parent organization's responsibility/liability in terms of tax reporting, auditing, etc.? To whom do the bank accounts really belong?

Interrelationships

This is a matter of situational management. If you are working with a strong, viable auxiliary that raises lots of money for your organization, certain ways of interacting will derive from the situation. Also, if the auxiliary is clearly focused solely on fundraising, it is easy to draw the line between auxilian volunteers and in-house, direct service volunteers. In fact, in that type of separation, any auxilian who *also* wants to become involved in direct service should be interviewed and placed into a volunteer assignment through the volunteer program office, as would any other volunteer. When working on-site, that person would be a "patient escort," "docent," "clerical aide," or whatever volunteer title applies. Her or his additional role as an "auxilian" would not affect the in-house volunteer function.

In some facilities, the auxiliary runs the in-house volunteer program. This may be quite workable but avoid the requirement that anyone who wants to volunteer has to *join* the auxiliary. This is one way to perpetuate discrimination and tradition, especially if there are special criteria for becoming an auxiliary member. Perhaps more importantly, few auxiliaries are able to accommodate the type of volunteer who wants to come in for one month to re-catalogue your library or who is on-call to help with press releases when needed. These types of assignments are rarely filled by people seeking to join the auxiliary or wanting the additional social aspects of group activities.

As CEO, you can establish guidelines to assure that any qualified person wanting to offer volunteer help is encouraged to apply, rather than being turned down at the first contact because s/he does not qualify as an "auxilian."

The real challenge to you as executive is the situation in which you have a weak auxiliary and a growing, vital volunteer program. You will have to examine the possible risks involved in placing the auxiliary under the jurisdiction of the volunteer office in an effort either to retire the group or to build it up again.

Facilities in inner city areas have in recent years seen a trend in auxiliaries whose members never set foot in the actual agency—who prefer, in fact, to keep several miles between themselves and the concrete reality of the problems the facility is trying to address. Again, some of these volunteer groups are successful in raising a great deal of money through suburban "thrift" shops, debutante balls, etc. and receive publicity and status for their efforts. This fundraising is vital and should not be denigrated because the volunteers disassociate themselves from the recipients of service. However, it is only fair to give comparable credit to those volunteers who, though not wealthy contributors, are willing to come on-site, roll up their sleeves and work directly with daily service delivery. This type of personal involvement deserves some status, too.

Given today's volunteerism climate, the concept of an auxiliary only makes sense if you feel that you want to maintain a fundraising group with a sense of unity. The social aspects of auxiliaries are indeed important to accomplishing the work, for many fundraising events require long hours of service and it is much more pleasant to volunteer in the company of friends. But you should expect the auxiliary to set goals, submit reports, and make a visible contribution. As the top administrator, you establish the standards. Auxilian volunteers deserve to know how they can be of most help, just as other types of volunteers should be recognized for their equally vital contributions to the organization.

ADVISORY COUNCILS

As with boards of directors and auxiliaries, advisory councils are special categories of volunteers with direct relationship to you as the CEO. If you are heading a unit of government, you may be working with a legally mandated advisory council including some or all members appointed by political leaders. Or you may have a council voluntarily established by your agency to gain more community input. Either way, members of your advisory council will respond most productively to motivating behavior on your part.

Clear expectations are imperative. Just because you have an "advisory" council does not mean that anyone has promised to use the advice given! Take the time to define exactly what the role of the advisory group is—and what it is not. Do not imply power when there is none. Most advisory groups have an impact through influence and persuasion, rather than through decision-making authority.

For this reason, it is good to avoid the use of the word "board" in relation to advisors. When someone joins a group called the "Advisory Board," there may be an implication of authority well beyond anything intended. Designations such as "Advisory Council" or "Community Representative Task Force" are more accurate.

Using the Principles of Volunteer Management

Recruitment of members onto an advisory council should be done with the same consideration as the recruitment of any other volunteers. Criteria for membership should be determined and a process instituted for interviewing, screening and orienting candidates and new members. A written job description for each member, with additional tasks for council officers, is also a critical tool. The director of volunteers can be of assistance to you in this process, just as described in working effectively with the board of directors.

Getting the Best Advice

If you have an advisory council, utilize it. People who have volunteered prefer to be activated than to see their names used on letterhead for political clout, without having had any input into what the organization is doing.

One of the obstacles to genuine involvement of advisory councils is the feeling that the only way to activate them is to call a group meeting. Ironically, full council meetings tend to work contrary to the goal of getting advice. Most advisors have been recruited because they "represent" a specific constituency: an ethnic group, neighborhood, profession, funding source, etc. In a group meeting, these very different people attempt to reach consensus on issues. In the process of reaching consensus, special interest, minority opinions are overlooked or played down. But, as executive, it is often those minority opinions that you most wanted advice about!

There are two ways to counteract this tendency to make the advisory council function as a group. One is to ask advisor volunteers to provide service in two distinct ways: participate in one or two group meetings of the full advisory council per year, and spend a few hours consulting with you one-to-one. Sometimes what you need is the perspective of someone with a very specific point of view. You can only gain this information individually— group meetings will dilute the opinions of any one particular advisor.

The other way to assure the benefit of many diverse points of view is to make sure advisory council meetings never take a vote. Taking a vote implies that the council can make policy, which it cannot, so allowing the majority to express only one opinion is misleading anyway. Instead of trying to distill all members' perspectives into one, try the following:

> —get the council to list all the *pros and cons* of any idea under discussion;

> —have the group generate a list of all the *questions* they can think of in reaction to a particular issue (sometimes a good question is more valuable than a lengthy statement of opinion);

> —ask for the minutes to reflect the *"minority opinion,"* just as the Supreme Court will publish the perspective of those judges who disagree with the ruling of the Court;

> —ask council members to suggest community *resources* that might assist with a particular project.

This type of approach gives you a great deal of advice that you can *use* and also makes advisor volunteers feel recognized for their input.

If your advisory council has been selected for its high degree of professional expertise, you may occasionally want the group to give you the benefit of their specific knowledge and "instruct" you on what course of action to take. In such special cases, taking a vote may be desirable. But differentiate between those situations in which you want general advice and those in which you are, in essence, delegating decision making. Otherwise, the advisors will assume that all their input carries the weight of giving instructions, which is probably not the case.

Finally, be sure everyone understands the difference between the roles of the advisory council and the organization's board of directors. Lines of authority can quickly become blurred, especially if you routinely encourage volunteers such as past board presidents to continue their service to your agency by joining the advisory council. Because you are the one person with a leadership role in both groups, you can demonstrate the differences between them by the way you plan each set of agendas, deliver reports to each group, and so on.

LEGAL ISSUES

Some of the issues that arise from the involvement of volunteers relate to questions of law. There are real legal concerns regarding the liability of and for volunteers, while other issues are quasi-legal in nature. Because of the seriousness of such questions, they require executive involvement.

Control

Whether stated directly or not, many of the questions asked about volunteers center on the concern for control. Legitimately, administrators want to be confident that their staff members provide services in accordance with the policies of the organization. Such confidence is bolstered by the belief that there is a clearly understood system of rewards for doing the job right and consequences for doing it wrong.

When managing employees, "rewards" available include a pay raise, a promotion, more vacation time, or some other tangible demonstration of positive recognition. "Consequences" are also tangible and range from withholding a pay raise to the ultimate threat of termination of employment. In the last analysis, both top executives and line workers feel that it is the threat of being fired—the mere possibility of it—that keeps employees "in line."

This is the crux of the debate about volunteers and control. What threat can an organization hold over the head of a volunteer that is as controlling as losing one's income?

But this question reflects a number of interesting attitudes. First, it indicates the managerial perspective that the threat of punishment is the best motivator for generating good work. Second, it confuses the available punishment with a guarantee of *prevention* of some unwanted behavior. And third, it neglects the important fact that the initial reasons for why the volunteer chose to come to the agency had nothing to do with a salary.

Managerially, it is more effective to govern through rewards than through negative consequences. Recognizing and visibly showing appreciation for work done right is far more motivating to everyone on staff than responding only to negative acts. Clearly, it is possible to reward volunteers in a variety of tangible ways similar to recognition of employees, including promotion to more responsible assignments.

For some salaried workers, the fear of being fired or even of a lesser consequence will indeed stop them from doing something wrong. But the person who no longer cares about the agency, is too weak to resist temptation, or believes him/herself clever enough to avoid detection will act despite any threat to his/her job. Also, many acts you as an administrator may consider "wrong," may be done in innocence, out of ignorance, or through strong personal convictions that happen to differ from the agency position. It is therefore a delusion to think that it is possible to prevent wrong doing through the threat of punishment.

The best way to feel confident about control of the organization's service providers is to start with careful screening of employees—and volunteers—at the time they apply to the organization. This includes clarifying expectations on both sides, particularly about any areas of service that might involve philosophic points of view. Another tool to assure compliance with agency rules is training. Both employees and volunteers deserve full instruction on how to do their jobs in the best way. This whole process is then reinforced by supervision and evaluation, including positive recognition for doing the job well. Even with this approach, prevention of problems cannot be guaranteed, but the likelihood of wrong doing is not determined by who receives a salary and who does not.

Finally, since money is not the reason why volunteers joined your organization in the first place, why should anyone miss having the control tool of threatening to take away money? If a volunteer cares a great deal about participating in your organization, then the most effective "threat" would be to no longer allow the person to volunteer. Yes, this means it is possible to "fire" a volunteer. The punishment is not losing an income, it is losing the chance to be involved.

Some administrators harbor the nightmare that if they tried to fire a volunteer, that person would simply say: "You can't tell me to leave, I'm a volunteer." First, the chances of this happening are so remote that it should never stop you from terminating a volunteer. The person who tries to argue with you probably has some other problem, be it an ax to grind or mental illness. Most healthy people would never stay in a place where they were no longer wanted. Second, from a legal standpoint, you do indeed have the right to designate who will be an agent of your organization—whether salaried or not. Under any circumstance, document the reasons for firing the volunteer, just as you would do with an employee.

In short, control is really not dependent upon paying a salary. Your best management approach for paid staff and volunteers alike is to motivate through approval.

This subject is closely linked to control and, in fact, is often raised as a smokescreen to hide the underlying fear that volunteers are

Confidentiality

uncontrollable. Confidentiality is an important and serious issue, but it is a *training* issue, not one tied to salaried versus voluntary employment.

Volunteers should be screened and trained to understand the meaning of client confidentiality and the necessity of maintaining it. In fact, violation of confidentiality should be stated as cause for immediate dismissal. However, whether or not a person gossips has nothing whatsoever to do with level of salary. Volunteers are no more prone to speak about a case outside of the agency than are salaried staff. In fact, the probability may even be less. Volunteers rarely discuss their volunteer work with their friends (one of the reasons why so many members of the public harbor the mistaken belief that no one volunteers any more!), while salaried staff, especially those in various professions, are more likely to describe the happenings of their week in a social context. This is also due to the fact that volunteers come in contact with clients for a few hours a week, while employees spend 40 hours with the agency's consumers. So who has more to talk about?

Any agent of the organization deserves to have access to whatever records or information are necessary in order to accomplish her/his assigned tasks. Conversely, this means that no one should be allowed to peruse records not relevant to an assigned case or to "eavesdrop" on other workers' activities. Both of these principles should apply equally to employees and volunteers. You do not give any and all employees access to client records. For example, the maintenance department would hardly have a good reason to read counseling records. Just as you are able to differentiate which employees may be given confidential information, you can select which volunteers require such data to complete their assignments.

If a volunteer is given a job to do that involves a particular client, it undercuts all chance for success to deny that volunteer access to the necessary background information. Much of this stems from suspicion that somehow the volunteer is "dabbling" in providing service and only the serious (i.e., salaried) worker should know the full story. Remember that this book makes the assumption that you have made sure all volunteers are appropriately selected and matched only to assignments that they are capable of fulfilling.

If you still have some doubts, ask the client for permission to reveal records to the volunteer. However you chose to handle this issue, the end result must be that you stand behind the volunteer as a legitimate representative of your organization.

Questions of Law

At various points in this book, I have indicated issues that may require seeking the advice of your organization's lawyer, accountant, or other expert consultants. We have reached a subject for which I decided to practice what I preach! The following pages were written by Jeffrey Kahn, an Associate here at Energize, while a law student at the University of Pennsylvania. Jeffrey has spent the last year researching legal issues related to volunteers and his article on "Organizations' Liability for Torts of Volunteers" appears in Volume 133 of the University of Pennsylvania Law Review, *July 1985, p. 1433.*

There are a variety of important legal issues relating to volunteers. Since laws vary from State to State and from time to time, our purpose here is not to provide any absolute answers to legal questions. Rather, the following pages will articulate some of the questions—and not even all of the questions—you might raise with your organization's lawyers. Only a full discussion with your attorney will give you specific information about the laws that apply to your volunteer program and help you to consider, in advance, what legal concerns might arise.

Keep in mind that discussions of potential legal problems always center on "worst case" scenarios. As you weigh your options for the utilization of volunteers, objectively analyze the range of difficult situations that could occur, and the likelihood of their occurrence. Consider each volunteer assignment category separately. Are the possible problems (and their potential cost) so great that they begin to offset the benefits your organization derives from various volunteer activities? In most cases you will probably conclude that the net effect of volunteer involvement is positive enough to justify working with volunteers, though you might take precautions to prevent the occurrence of any "worst case" situation.

Most legal questions pertaining to volunteers apply equally to salaried employees. Just as you do not allow complex potential legal difficulties to inhibit you from hiring salaried personnel, the existence of similar legal questions should not become a roadblock to the utilization of volunteers.

The two broad areas of law which concern any employer are "contracts" and "torts." Contract law concerns the promises and obligations of parties to each other. Torts concern wrongful acts that result in injury to another party. "Injury" is a broad term that covers consequences beyond actual physical harm.

The Employer/Employee Relationship

Earlier in this book we suggested that you consider volunteers as your nonsalaried personnel department. That characterization is useful in thinking about legal issues as well as managerial ones, since most legal doctrines governing "employees" and "employers" do not explicitly require that the employee receive a salary.

You may hear three sets of terms being used to describe the possible relationships between your agency and its salaried workers/volunteers: employer/employee; master/servant; and principal/agent. Each of these sets has a different legal meaning, but all may be pertinent in some way to defining the extent of connection between your agency and its volunteers.

In terms of contract law, the relevant issues involve whether the volunteer is able to act on behalf of the agency and thus obligate or legally bind the agency to do something. When a volunteer acts, under your control, to further the work of the organization, s/he may be seen as your legal representative or "agent." The extent of the volunteer's legal capacity as agent is limited by the "authority" given by the organization, but such authority may be presumed by certain organizational actions, not just through written or formal instructions. This all becomes especially relevant if volunteers are active in assignments involving third parties.

In terms of torts law, your organization may be liable for acts committed by volunteers who are handling assignments under your control and direction, and are therefore legally "servants" of your organization as "master."

Liability Issues

In fact, the most important legal issues related to volunteers involve the law of liabilities, or "torts." You are undoubtedly familiar with some of these liability issues since your organization probably has some insurance for personal or property damage. This section will explore some of the various legal questions relating to liability: the liability of your organization for damage caused by volunteers, the liability of your organization for injuries suffered by volunteers, and other liability issues including indemnification of board members.

Liability for Acts of Volunteers

Until recently, most nonprofit organizations were not liable for harm caused by anyone working for the organization, whether salaried or not, but were protected by a legal doctrine called "charitable immunity." Most States have now abolished this shield from liability, and nonprofit organizations are now liable for damage caused by any of the organization's workers, just as any business would be liable.

There is a general legal principle that a master is liable for injuries caused by his or her servant during the servant's performance of his or her work. Courts apply this doctrine (called *respondeat superior*) to employers and hold them fully liable for damage caused by an employee on the job. Recently, a number of States have also applied this doctrine to instances in which a volunteer caused the damage.

In order for your organization to be liable for damage caused by a volunteer, three conditions must be met:

—the volunteer must have negligently or intentionally caused the damage;

—the volunteer must have been performing his or her assigned work at the time of the accident;

—the volunteer must have been a "servant" of the organization, that is, within the control of the organization.

All three of these requirements involve complex legal concepts which vary from State to State, and which your lawyer can define more fully. The bottom line, however, is that in most States your organization would be fully liable for any harm caused by a volunteer participating in a structured volunteer program, regardless of how careful your management or supervision.

Anticipating Potential Liability

While the above summary of the law may surprise some readers, this is no different than the law for salaried employees. Rather than risk having to pay the full cost of damage accidently caused by a volunteer (such damages awarded by a court can be considerable), most employers of salaried and nonsalaried servants take two types of precautions. First, they engage in management practices which help reduce the chance of accidents ever occurring, which is called "risk management." Second, they purchase insurance which will pay for the damage in the event an accident does occur.

Your organization probably practices some degree of risk management already. For example, you may require employees or volunteers to have certain experience or training before performing specific tasks. Requiring that a volunteer have a lifesaving certificate before being assigned to conduct a swimming program is a form of risk management, since certified lifeguards are more apt to take the necessary safety measures than those without such formal training. Risk management involves anticipating the most likely ways a volunteer could accidentally cause damage, and then devising reasonable and cost-effective ways to reduce the likelihood of these accidents. Preventive techniques include requiring special training or education of volunteers, ensuring proper supervision of volunteers, and screening volunteers for certain personality traits (responsibility, maturity, ability to handle stress, etc.). Written job descriptions for volunteers play an important role in risk management.

It is of course essential that you have some liability insurance to cover damage caused by volunteers, and you should check to see what your current policy covers. It is important that your insurance *explicitly* covers damage caused by volunteers. Many insurance companies are reluctant to cover volunteers, since they believe organizations do not have sufficient control over volunteer actions. They may even imply—based purely on prejudice about volunteers—that being a volunteer is in some way connected to the likelihood of causing damage. You should therefore be prepared for this attitude when talking to your insurance agent and be ready to explain the steps your organization takes to properly train and supervise volunteers. With volunteers, as with salaried employees, you will need to weigh the cost of insuring certain activities against the benefits you derive from these activities.

Liability for Injuries to Volunteers

A volunteer who gets injured may attempt to recover medical or other costs from the organization. Whether the volunteer is entitled to such compensation depends on the circumstances surrounding the accident and whether the organization or any of its servants acted in a negligent manner. This situation is, for legal purposes, just like that in which a client or other third party is injured by the volunteer. Once again, you should check to see if your insurance covers this situation.

One way to reduce the chances of your organization being sued for injury suffered by a volunteer is to have the volunteer sign a waiver of liability. In consulting with your lawyer about the usefulness of a liability waiver, you should realize that such waivers are often not as effective as they might seem. A waiver only operates as a bar to legal action if it can be shown that the signer fully understood the risk involved and the meaning of the waiver. Even so, a waiver may be useful because it provides an opportunity to discuss possible risks with the volunteers, and because some volunteers will honor the waiver agreement and not sue in the event of injury.

The volunteer who gets injured may have other sources of compensation, such as personal insurance, which would make it unnecessary to proceed against your organization. However, you may want to provide insurance coverage to volunteers. Most often, such insurance provides for payment only in "excess" of other coverage available. In some states, certain categories of volunteers are covered under Workers Compensation plans. Again, check with your lawyer to find out about the specific requirements of your State's law.

Car Insurance

If volunteer assignments involve driving a motor vehicle, be sure to check appropriate insurance coverage. Though the specific concerns may be affected by whether the volunteers are authorized to drive an agency car or van, or utilize their private vehicles, liability is an issue in both cases.

Board Member Indemnification

Members of your board of directors can be liable for various "errors" or "omissions" committed in the line of decision-making for the organization. In recognition of this, many organizations have purchased insurance to indemnify their board in case the individual members are named in a suit. Indemnification simply means that the insurer will cover the costs of any lawsuit and will pay any damages awarded, within agreed-upon limits. You should check on when board members can be sued in your State, and should investigate insurance options.

Liability of the Director of Volunteers

One other liability question often raised is whether the director of volunteers or other supervisor of volunteers can be liable in the event a volunteer causes an injury or is injured. There is no special legal doctrine covering this situation, but someone can be sued whenever s/he negligently contributes to an injury.

Fair Labor   The Fair Labor Standards Act (29
Standards Act   U.S.C.A. Section 201 *et seq.*) has
                        recently been extended to apply to
                        government units as well as to cer-
tain businesses and nonprofit organizations. It regulates a range of
employer/employee transactions, including how overtime is to be
calculated and remunerated. It basically considers any time that an
employee works over and above 40 hours a week to be overtime,
requiring overtime pay.

Nonprofit and government agencies usually have a dedi-
cated staff of employees, many of whom care enough about the
work they do to willingly—and voluntarily—give extra hours to
the organization. Such volunteer time is spent in activities ranging
from special individualized attention to patients to assisting with a
holiday party. Clearly, in light of the Fair Labor Standards Act, this
poses a serious question for volunteerism.

How can an employee who also wishes to volunteer be
enabled to do so, without the employer risking a suit for overtime
pay? The narrowest interpretation of the Fair Labor Standards Act
would answer that no employee can ever be a "volunteer" as
well—all time over 40 hours should be paid as overtime. However,
this has not been tested sufficiently in the courts. At this point, the
best advice would be to use the following guidelines:

1. Be sure that no pressure—overt or implied—is given to
   make an employee feel that extra time is "expected." It
   should be a free choice to volunteer.

2. Insist that the employee "apply" for a volunteer position,
   filling out a volunteer application form and going
   through the volunteer office for placement. The
   employee should sign in and out on the volunteer attendance form, separate from any employee time logs.

3. The assignment the volunteer carries should be demon-
   strably different from the job description of the person's
   salaried position.

By taking care to keep the volunteering distinct from any
salaried responsibilities, you will be in a better position to defend
any possible suit.

All of these legal issues raise com- **Resolve Concerns**
plex questions which an attorney
can help you fully understand and
resolve. Such consultation should
help you to anticipate possible legal problems before they arise
and to strengthen the way your organization involves volunteers.

EVALUATION OF VOLUNTEER IMPACT

Because you expend time, money and other resources on the involvement of volunteers, it is clearly good management practice to evaluate whether this expense is worth it. It also should be of interest to assess what volunteers accomplish and how well they do it. In fact, this assessment is of equal interest to the volunteers themselves, since no one wants to give time to do something that has no impact.

Some agencies routinely overlook the volunteer component when they do an internal evaluation study. As CEO, you can see to it that services provided by volunteers are evaluated with the same concern as those delivered by employees.

What to Assess

One of the most uncreative—and unhelpful—questions posed to volunteer program leaders is: "how many volunteers do we have and how many hours did they give us this year?" Unfortunately, this is too often the extent of program "evaluation" for the volunteer component. A tally of hours served without analysis of what was accomplished and how well it was done is not worth compiling. It is a left-handed compliment to assume that somehow the importance of volunteer involvement is self-evident. It is up to the top executive to require some demonstration of the value of volunteers.

One of the problems in evaluating volunteer achievement is that certain types of volunteer assignments require services that are described in terms of their quality, rather than their quantity. Indeed, the titles given to some of these assignments reflect the inherent "how-can-we-ever-measure-this?" aspect of the work:

"friendly" visitor; Big "Brother"; victim "support" counselor. In reality, it is quite possible to determine some identifiable benchmarks of achievement, regardless of the assignment. Such indicators may be a bit subjective, but both the recipient and the giver of service should be able to point to successes such as: the client makes a point of asking the volunteer's advice on something; the teenager goes to school regularly for two months; the patient's family identifies an increase in morale.

It is equally difficult to evaluate the efforts of salaried staff in services designed to affect the "quality of life" for recipients. Accountability and evaluation are nevertheless sought after by all types of social service agencies, so the challenge of finding ways to assess the impact of volunteer efforts may have implications for other service evaluation as well.

If measurable goals and objectives are articulated for the volunteer program at the start of the period under evaluation, it will obviously be possible to ask whether these were met. An evaluation (probably annually) should analyze performance in several areas:

1. The actual quantity and quality of the work done by volunteers—preferably in each assignment category.

2. The accomplishments of the volunteer management team, including such overview questions as the demographic makeup of the volunteer corps, number and type of recruitment outreach efforts, etc.

3. The type and degree of service provided to the salaried staff by volunteers and/or the volunteer program office.

4. The benefits to the organization as a whole from volunteer involvement.

Some of the questions that could be asked to assess the contribution of volunteers in a given period are similar to those that would be asked about the work of salaried staff. In addition, consider some of the following approaches to identifying the value of volunteers:

—Have our consumers expressed any awareness of, appreciation for, or comments about volunteers here?

—What were we able to do more of this year than last because of the extra help from volunteers?

—What did volunteers free staff to do?

—What were we able to innovate or experiment with this year because volunteers agreed to test something new?

—In which assignments did we have the most turnover and why? Which assignments are the most popular with volunteers and why?

—Has our public relations or image changed and can we trace any of this change to the impact of volunteers?

—Is our volunteer corps representative of the community we serve?

—Have members of the salaried staff visibly developed their supervisory skills as a result of working with volunteers?

These are the kinds of questions that will provide information immediately translatable into management decisions. The data gathered can be used to uncover training needs, recruitment strategies, service deserving recognition, etc.

Comparisons

There is one danger worth mentioning. Be cautious of drawing comparisons between the work of volunteers and that of salaried staff. As you are already aware, this book recommends making sure that the job descriptions of volunteers differ tangibly from those of employees. If you follow this advice, it will always be clear that you are evaluating each group separately, based on the different assignments they are each handling.

However, we have also already identified one major reason why volunteers are threatening to salaried staff: the fear that, if volunteers do well, it will raise questions about the role played by employees. When reporting the results of any evaluation, therefore, it is helpful to praise the good work of both groups—and also to indicate areas of weakness/need for improvement of both groups.

At times there are reasons to do some comparing between the service provided solely by salaried staff and the service provided by a combination of effort by employees and volunteers. This is important if you are trying, for example, to measure the impact of one-to-one volunteers assisting juvenile probationers. One way to do the measuring would be to compare the rate of recidivism of probationers without an adult volunteer friend to those with a volunteer. While this is a very reasonable evaluation approach, recognize that it could *imply* something about the abilities of the various probation officers, too. Here is an excellent example of how the wording of the final evaluation report can help or hurt volunteer/salaried staff relationships.

Ongoing Assessment: Volunteer Program Reports

Apart from an annual or periodic evaluation of the volunteer program, you should be looking for indicators all year round for whether volunteers are being effective—and whether your organization is providing the most supportive working environment for volunteers. This means requiring reports from the director of volunteers with the same frequency as you require them from other department heads, probably monthly. The data in these reports will be compiled from statistics being maintained in the volunteer office, but also from reports submitted to the director of volunteers by the various departments in which volunteers operate. You can also ask each department to include the accomplishments of volunteers in their unit directly to you within their monthly report. (This is another way to demonstrate that you are interested.)

Among the things to look for in regular reports are such data as the rate of turnover in specific assignment categories, accomplishments of short-term versus long-term volunteers, and assignments that have been vacant for an unusually long time. The data may alert you to trouble spots. If turnover seems to occur monthly in a particular unit, perhaps there is a problem with the supervisory staff or the physical environment there.

As with all data, the numbers alone do not tell the whole story. Some statistics reflect normal variables in the operation of a volunteer program, such as anticipated high rates of turnover in a particular month (such as students leaving in June). Vacancies may demonstrate the careful screening being done by the director of volunteers, who is willing to allow vacancies for a time rather than to fill a slot with inappropriate volunteers. See if the report includes information on recruitment efforts focused on the unfilled assignment categories and if the number of screening interviews of applicants is higher than the number of new volunteers actually brought on board.

The director of volunteers also has the responsibility of giving you information about volunteers that is useful to you in your work as executive. At any given time, you should know the answers to the following questions:

—What is the "profile" of the volunteers in your facility? Specifically:
    —what is the range of ages represented?
    —the percentage of men and women?
    —their racial distribution?
    —the neighborhoods they represent?

—*Exactly* what do volunteers do?

—Do they perform these roles successfully? (by what criteria?)

—Which units in the agency do not utilize volunteers? Why not?

—Where there is the highest turnover of volunteers, and why?

—How many public relations and community contacts are made weekly by the Volunteer Department, with which organizations or individuals, and with what results?

—What suggestions or observations are being made by volunteers that might be useful to agency management?

If the director of volunteers is not already supplying you with this type of data, ask for it. Think about how much more useful such data is than the so-called bottom line figure of "how many volunteers do we have?"

If you are computerizing your organization's records, plan to include the volunteer office's records as well. But be sure that your computer programmers talk with the director of volunteers before formatting the record files. Unless you are on-line with an interactive system, the computer will only be useful for storage of information about past volunteer efforts. This can help generate reports at the end of the month, but on a daily basis, the director of volunteers handles fluid data that changes with the current schedules and activities of volunteers.

Evaluating the Director of Volunteers

Though it is reasonably obvious, it does not hurt to point out that the evaluation of the volunteer program is not the same thing as an evaluation of your director of volunteers. You are justified in assessing the competence and achievements of the director of volunteers by examining the way in which the volunteer program is managed, but the achievements of the *volunteers* themselves are not necessarily the reflection—nor the fault—of the leader of the program.

A great deal depends on your expectations of what the position of director of volunteers means to your agency. If you set your sights low and only want a volunteer program "maintained," then you do not need much in the way of creativity or vision from your director of volunteers. If you recognize the potential of this component of your service delivery, you will want the leader to be a full participatory member of your administrative team.

Leland Kaiser, an authority in hospital management, has an interesting point of view about what an executive should expect from *any* department head. He challenges CEOs to require every department head, on an annual basis, to report on the major trends and issues affecting his/her area of specialty. Kaiser's point is that leadership involves not only day-to-day management, but also continuing education about developments in the outside world that will impact on your operations.

You should hold the director of volunteers responsible for keeping informed about volunteerism in general. S/he is, as already indicated, your in-house expert on volunteers. Is s/he truly aware of what is happening with citizen participation in other settings? Can s/he express long-range goals for the volunteer program and predict changes that will occur in the future? Is s/he aware of trends in your organization's specific field (medicine, recreation, child welfare, etc.) and how these might affect your needs for volunteer involvement in the future?

Individual Volunteer Evaluations

Yes, it is legitimate and reasonable to evaluate the individual performance of volunteers—providing that volunteers know in advance that there will be periodic assessment, that it is done equitably for all volunteers, and that it is based on having told each volunteer what was expected from him or her in the first place (the job description). In fairness, the evaluation should be a two-way process, also allowing the volunteer the chance to give feedback on the support received from the organization.

It is more than semantics to call the volunteer evaluation a "progress report" or "future action plan." This sounds less judgmental and emphasizes moving forward rather than simply looking back. In this way, the mutual assessment process can re-motivate everyone.

Making Changes

As with any program evaluation, it is only worth the effort if you are willing to analyze the results of the assessment and develop plans to implement necessary changes. If done correctly, an evaluation will point out areas of strength as well as of weakness, since improvement might come simply from doing more of what has been done right in the past. From the volunteer management perspective, the importance of evaluation is the need to be sure that volunteers are assigned to work that genuinely requires attention. Otherwise, volunteer effort is wasted on activities that are not useful. There is too much to be done to permit that.

THE DOLLAR VALUE
OF VOLUNTEERS

Evaluating volunteer program effectiveness provides you with information helpful in your administrative responsibilities. But so far we have only discussed the evaluation of volunteer activities, not the assessment of the financial value of volunteer involvement. This chapter presents a method available to you as executive for becoming more aware of the real cost of operating your organization.

Just as you should involve your accountant or finance officer in financial considerations, I, too, have asked my CPA to participate in writing this chapter. The following pages have been written by John Paul Dalsimer, CPA, who has extensive experience working with a wide variety of nonprofit organizations on their accounting and organizational questions. He is a founder and past president of Accountants for the Public Interest, a national association that encourages accountants to participate in community service. For ten years he served on the Pennsylvania Commission on Charitable Organizations, which oversees charitable solicitations in Pennsylvania.

Almost all nonprofit organizations receive in-kind contributions and the donation of time from a board of directors and other volunteers. Office space, printing, postage and a variety of other in-kind services are often donated to nonprofits. All of these are of great importance to program services and all have a dollar value.

Unfortunately, most nonprofits ignore such contributions on their financial statements—both those for internal use and those for external dissemination. In order for you to know how much it *really* costs to run your organization, a dollar value should be placed on volunteer time and in-kind contributions. These are as valuable as cash contributions.

Generally, volunteers are simply not mentioned on agency financial statements. This omission tends to *de*-value their services. To report that it cost $7,200 to winterize ten homebound elderly peoples' homes without mentioning the $4,000 *worth* of volunteer services or the $2,000 *worth* of donated supplies is to reach some false conclusions about the actual cost of the service. From a management perspective, never having to "account" for the utilization of volunteers can result in wasting volunteer effort or in discounting its cost to the volunteer and its value to the organization.

The premise of this chapter can be summed up in the following formula:

> *Actual expenses* plus *the value of contributed time and materials equals the* true cost of service.

Whether or not you wish to adopt all the steps of the method presented here, you may well want to consider how you can be certain that you (and your board or other decision-makers) base your planning on the most accurate picture of your resource expenditures.

Some of what I am about to present is "radical" in that it goes beyond what traditional accounting practices require at the present time. Therefore, also included is a section to prepare you for discussing all of this with your accountant. However, I emphasize that most of the ideas in this chapter can be comfortably used immediately and, in fact, reflect current accounting standards for nonprofit organizations and Federal income tax law.

Why Compute Our True Costs?

You may be thinking, "I'm not sure we want to know the full cost of our program . . . We certainly don't want anyone else to compare how much our program really costs versus another program." Maybe you don't—but you as the administrator, and your board of directors, should be aware of the full costs of operating.

Clearly there are some philosophic issues at stake here. For example, some might argue that almost all nonprofits utilize volunteers as an inherent part of their operations. Such donated services are therefore "assumed" and there is no need to keep track of their dollar value. Furthermore, if people are willing to volunteer their time to an organization, should the value of that time be measured? Or is the volunteering itself "proof of the value of the program"? The argument includes the belief that it is hard to keep records anyway and the expense of doing so cannot be justified.

Another issue relates to the "bottom line." Profit-making organizations have the "bottom line" of whether or not they make a profit. Sales are the measure of whether the public thinks the company is making a desired product or providing a worthwhile service. Should nonprofits be treated differently? If a social good is being provided, should cost be considered?

Also, should one nonprofit be compared to another on the basis of how much money each spends to provide its services? Should an alcohol rehabilitation program be compared to another alcohol rehabilitation program on any basis other than the effectiveness of its rehabilitation?

An additional problem is that valuing donated time and materials and adding them to income on your financial statements will increase the apparent size of the organization. Will this be seen as an attempt to inflate the figures to make the agency look bigger than it is? Might it affect how some grant makers compute your overhead allowance? Or, will it have the effect of making the agency appear "rich" because of its available resources? Will such conclusions make potential donors think you do not need their money?

None of these questions has an easy answer, but I do suggest you should be keeping track of your donated time and materials.

Why?

Your board of directors and funding sources, both current and potential, are interested in what your resources are and how you use them . . . and donated time and materials are a very significant resource. Properly presented, inclusion of donated time and materials on your financial statements should impress potential funders with the degree of support demonstrated by the community—and with your managerial sophistication at recognizing the value of such support. Funding sources will see the value of volunteer service as "leverage" for their money. The funder's dollar contribution to your program has the potential to generate two, five or twenty times its worth through the value of volunteer time and in-kind materials. For each one dollar a donor contributes, you are providing four, five or twenty dollars worth of service. But you can only make this point if you keep records of donated time and materials and put a dollar value on them.

Certain donors and government grantmaking agencies will accept volunteer time as in-kind "matching funds" on grant applications. Again, you will need to be able to document any value you place on such contributed services.

There are internal management reasons for wanting to keep records on volunteers, too. You need to be able to recognize and thank volunteers. It is hard to know what you are thanking them for if you do not know how many hours they have given. It is much more meaningful to thank someone for 105 hours, or for five hours a week for ten weeks, than for "all your time." Mentioning specific results and end products is also important.

I suggest that you keep records of volunteer time and determine a dollar value for that time, at least to be used for internal purposes. You may, initially, decide not to record the value in your accounting records. At a minimum, making a start at valuing the contributions of volunteers should give you and your board a more significant and valid picture of the cost of human effort you expend in delivering services.

Keeping Track of Donated Time

How do you keep track of donated time? The method is very similar to how you keep track of time for which you pay: by using time sheets of various kinds.[1] It is also important, for accounting purposes, to have all staff members (paid and unpaid) allocate their recorded time, at least by: 1) each major program or service category; 2) management and general administration; and 3) fundraising. This information is needed to prepare your financial statements and the report to the Federal government (Form 990), both of which require that expenses be broken out into these categories (at a minimum).

Once you have recorded accumulated volunteer hours, you can calculate their value by multiplying hours by an appropriate hourly rate for each of the jobs performed.

One of the objections often raised about keeping track of volunteer hours is that it is difficult, if not impossible, to get volunteers in *all* categories to keep a record of the time they contribute. This may be true, but the solution is to aim for recording as much of the time as possible, not to ignore recording some because you cannot record all. You can begin to apply the following valuation system to whatever number of hours you have gathered for volunteer service.

Dollar Value of Volunteers

Most administrators are justifiably concerned with measuring the "cost effectiveness" of agency projects—whether the funds and staff time expended are commensurate with the value of the service provided. Cost effectiveness is easy to prove for a volunteer program. The actual cost of salarying the program staff, paying for supplies, and other expenses is "leverage" money that produces many multiples of hours of volunteer service than that same amount of money could have "paid" for hours of employee time. (However, this argument is only valid if the evaluation of the quality of volunteer service concludes that something meaningful was produced!)

In order to generate the most useful data, take the time to estimate the dollar value as fairly as possible. Do *not* fall into the common trap of using the minimum wage or the national median wage as a basis for your computation. The vast majority of volunteer assignments are worth a great deal more than minimum wage and probably more than the median, too. Averaging the salaries of all your employees to determine an "average" hourly rate does not compare similar jobs nor include the cost of employee benefits.

One other trap is to confuse the dollar value of the service provided by volunteers with the earning power of the people who are doing the volunteering. If someone earns his or her living as a lawyer, teacher, or doctor and volunteers to write a brief, teach classes, or do blood tests for your organization—then you are justified to claim the donated services at the hourly rate normally charged by that volunteer. But if that same lawyer, teacher or doctor volunteers to paint your rec hall, drive clients to a picnic, or play chess with residents—the dollar value of his or her volunteer work has nothing to do with his or her regular earning power. You must assess the value of each volunteer assignment based on what it would cost you to purchase that type of work in the marketplace.

The best system for determining the true dollar value of volunteer services has been proposed by G. Neil Karn at the Virginia Department of Volunteerism.[2] He details his approach at great length, but here are his key points:

TRUE DOLLAR VALUE OF VOLUNTEERS
WORKSHEET

Volunteer Job Title: _____

  I. Equivalent Salaried Job Classification
     (Based on a comparison of the tasks and responsibilities described in the volunteer job description with those of an equivalent employee)

     Equivalent Salaried Job Title: _____

 II. Annual Salary for Equivalent Salaried Classification: $_____

III. Value of Benefits Package:
     FICA $_____
     Health Insurance   _____
     Life Insurance   _____
     Workers Compensation Insurance   _____
     Retirement   _____
     Other Benefits: _____   _____
                       Total Value of Benefits: _____

 IV. Annual Salary **+** Benefits Package =
     TOTAL ANNUAL COMPENSATION PACKAGE: $_____

  V. Established Annual Work Hours for
     Agency: _____ hours/week × 52 weeks =   _____ hours

 VI. Hours Paid but Not Worked Annually:
     Annual Leave   _____hours
     Paid Holidays   _____
     Paid Sick Leave   _____
                       Total Hours Paid/Not Worked: _____

VII. Established Annual Hours **—** Hours
     Paid but Not Worked =
     ACTUAL WORK HOURS ANNUALLY: _____ hours

VIII. **TOTAL ANNUAL COMPENSATION PACKAGE ÷**
      ACTUAL WORK HOURS ANNUALLY =

      TRUE DOLLAR VALUE OF EACH
      HOUR OF VOLUNTEER TIME IN
      THIS JOB DESCRIPTION: $_____

1. It is possible to find an equivalent salaried job category for every volunteer assignment, even if it means a little creativity and searching. Each volunteer assignment should be given its own dollar equivalency, without trying to find an average rate for all volunteers helping the program.

2. The cost of paying an employee includes benefits that raise the total value of the "annual employee compensation package" considerably.

3. We routinely pay salaried staff for hours they do *not* work, while we credit volunteers only for hours they actually put in.

4. Volunteers should be "credited" with the dollar equivalent of the hourly amount an employee would earn for actual hours worked.

The illustration to the left shows the way to compute the actual value of volunteer services using the Karn method.

By using the volunteer job description for each assignment, it is possible to compare the tasks given to volunteers to those listed in the job descriptions for employees *somewhere*. This may require some research to identify paid job classifications. The local offices of the United States' and your State's Department of Labor maintain useful listings of job categories and pay scales in your geographic region. Some of the actual equivalent job categories in Virginia that Karn uses as examples are:

VOLUNTEER ASSIGNMENT	EQUIVALENT PAID CLASSIFICATION
Criminal justice one-to-one visitor	Probation and parole officer trainee
Volunteer member of a conference planning committee	Human resource developer
Little League coach	Playground supervisor
Little League official	Recreation specialist
Big Brother/Sister	Outreach worker
Board member	Executive Director

For some volunteer jobs, the equivalent paid classification will be more obvious. For example, a volunteer assigned to help with mass mailings and photocopying would be equivalent to an entry-level clerk or secretary position. A volunteer writing your newsletter would be equivalent to a public relations specialist or editor.

Also, you have the right to consider the qualifications of the volunteers. If someone comes to you with experience in the type of assignment s/he will carry, you are correct in computing that volunteer's dollar equivalent at higher than a "trainee" level. Similarly, if a volunteer has been with your organization for several years, that person's equivalent wage would be higher than a new volunteer's/employee's.

Once you have identified the equivalent paid classification and its annual salary, you next must add together the *benefits* package: FICA, retirement, insurances, and other benefits. Add this dollar amount to the salary and you have the "Annual Compensation Package" for an employee in that position.

Now compute how many *hours* a year your organization has established as expected work hours. For example, 40 hours per week times 52 weeks per year equals 2080 hours per year. Using this as a base, add up the hours for which employees are paid but do not work. This includes annual leave (vacation), paid holidays and paid sick leave. For many organizations, this can total over 200 hours per year. Now subtract this total from the established number of work hours to arrive at "Actual Work Hours Annually."

By dividing the Actual Work Hours Annually into the Annual Compensation Package, you arrive at the *"True Hourly Value."* It is *this* hourly rate that should be used in determining the dollar value of volunteer service. And as Karn says, this figure should be presented unapologetically!

Your Financial Records   Let's turn to how to record the dollar equivalency amount of volunteer service in your agency's financial records. It is really not different from how you record the salaries of paid staff. For example, Hometown Agency has several service programs, including Service Program X and Service Program Y. In a typical month, the accounting entry to record the cost of staff would look like this:

Service Program X—salaries	$3,600	
Service Program X—benefits	400	
Service Program Y—salaries	6,200	
Service Program Y—benefits	600	
Administration—salaries	900	
Administration—benefits	100	
Cash		$8,700
Withheld Payroll Taxes		2,000
Benefits		1,100

I realize that, in most cases, this entry would come directly from the Payroll Register, but I have displayed it in this format to make the example clear.

Hometown Agency also utilizes volunteers in these program areas and uses the "true dollar value equivalency" formula just presented in this chapter. The entry the bookkeeper would make in the General Journal to record the value of the volunteers' contributed time would be:

Service Program X—donated time	$1,900	
Service Program Y—donated time	3,500	
Administration—donated time	400	
Contributions—donated time		$5,800

It should be noted that the value of the donated time is recorded as both an expense and a contribution. Yes, the effect on the "bottom line" is zero; the contribution is offset by the expenses. But, the *total of each category* is now correctly stated.

Why do I say "correctly stated"? If the entry for donated time is not made, it would appear that it cost only $4,000 that month to run Service Program X. But we know that it actually cost $5,900 worth of human energy to carry out this program.

Hometown Agency also includes volunteer time on its financial statements. The accompanying illustrations show part of Hometown's annual Statement of Support, Revenue, and Expenses and Statement of Functional Expenses. On the Statement of Support, Revenue, and Expenses, under Support and Revenue is a total of $43,000 in donated time. This $43,000 is also included in the section on Expenses, but does not appear as a separate item. To find it, look at the Statement of Functional Expenses. There you will see the $43,000 itemized within "Total Staff Expenses."

HOMETOWN AGENCY
STATEMENT OF SUPPORT, REVENUE, AND EXPENSES
and CHANGES IN FUND BALANCES
Year Ended December 31, 19X2
with Comparative Totals for 19X1

	19X2 Current Funds Unrestricted	Restricted	Total All Funds 19X2	19X1
Public support and revenue:				
Public support:				
Contributions	$352,000	$47,000	$399,000	$360,000
Special events (net of direct costs of $42,000 in 19X2 and $30,000 in 19X1)	40,000	—	40,000	39,000
	392,000	47,000	439,000	399,000
Donated time (note X)	**43,000**	**—**	**43,000**	**39,000**
Total public support	435,000	47,000	482,000	438,000
Revenue:				
Membership dues	8,000	—	8,000	5,000
Investment income	8,000	2,000	10,000	7,000
Miscellaneous	2,000	—	2,000	2,000
Total revenue	18,000	2,000	20,000	14,000
Total support and revenue	453,000	49,000	502,000	452,000
Expenses:				
Program services:				
Program X	76,000	—	76,000	64,000
Program Y	80,000	49,000	129,000	120,000
Professional education and training	49,000	—	49,000	45,000
Community services	50,000	—	50,000	45,000
Total program services	255,000	49,000	304,000	274,000
Supporting services:				
Management & general	87,000	—	87,000	83,000
Fundraising	67,000	—	67,000	60,000
Total supporting services	154,000	—	154,000	143,000
Total expenses	409,000	49,000	$458,000	$417,000
Excess (deficiency) of public support and revenue over expenses	44,000	(2,000)		
Fund balances, beginning of year	162,000	22,000		
Fund balances, end of year	$206,000	$20,000		

(See accompanying notes to financial statements)

In these two illustrations, "note X" would probably be included in the *Summary of Significant Accounting Policies,* explaining that donated time and materials are recorded on the financial records and the method of valuation used.

HOMETOWN AGENCY
STATEMENT OF FUNCTIONAL EXPENSES
Year Ended December 31, 19X2
with Comparative Totals for 19X1

| | Program Services | | | | | Supporting Services | | | Total Expenses | |
| | 19X2 | | | | | | | | | |
	Program X	Program Y	Prof. Educ. & Trng.	Community Services	Total	Management & General	Fund-raising	Total	19X2	19X1
Salaries	$35,000	$62,000	$25,000	$26,000	$148,000	$31,000	$36,000	$67,000	$215,000	$195,000
Donated time (note X)	**15,000**	**20,000**	**—**	**—**	**35,000**	**8,000**	**—**	**8,000**	**43,000**	**39,000**
Employee benefits	2,000	3,000	2,000	2,000	9,000	2,000	3,000	5,000	14,000	14,000
Payroll taxes, etc.	1,000	2,000	1,000	1,000	5,000	1,000	2,000	3,000	8,000	10,000
Total staff expenses	53,000	87,000	28,000	29,000	197,000	42,000	41,000	83,000	280,000	253,000
Professional fees	1,000	5,000	3,000	2,000	11,000	5,000	3,000	8,000	19,000	17,000
Supplies	2,000	3,000	3,000	3,000	11,000	7,000	5,000	12,000	23,000	25,000
Telephone	2,000	6,000	1,000	2,000	11,000	6,000	4,000	10,000	21,000	18,000
Postage	2,000	2,000	1,000	1,000	6,000	7,000	1,000	8,000	14,000	12,000
Occupancy	5,000	8,000	3,000	3,000	19,000	4,000	4,000	8,000	27,000	22,000
Rental of equipment	1,000	2,000	—	—	3,000	3,000	2,000	5,000	8,000	6,000
Local transportation	3,000	2,000	1,000	3,000	9,000	2,000	2,000	4,000	13,000	9,000
Printing & publications	4,000	5,000	4,000	4,000	17,000	2,000	1,000	3,000	20,000	24,000
Miscellaneous	1,000	4,000	2,000	2,000	9,000	2,000	2,000	4,000	13,000	12,000
Total expenses before depreciation	74,000	124,000	46,000	49,000	293,000	80,000	65,000	145,000	438,000	398,000
Depreciation of equipment	2,000	5,000	3,000	1,000	11,000	7,000	2,000	9,000	20,000	19,000
Total expenses	$76,000	$129,000	$49,000	$50,000	$304,000	$87,000	$67,000	$154,000	$458,000	$417,000

(See accompanying notes to financial statements)

**Your Financial
Reports**

You can adopt the same recording and reporting system as Hometown Agency for your organization. Once you begin to report on this basis, you, your board, and your funding sources will have the complete picture of your organization's resources.

No matter what, never use the phrase "volunteers *save* us money." This implies that you had funds that you did not need to spend because volunteers were on the scene. More accurate would be: "volunteers *extend* our budget beyond anything we would otherwise be able to afford."

Whatever methods you use to record donated time, you should save timesheets and computations. You will have to work with your bookkeeper, treasurer, and CPA to find the best way to do this for you. You may find that you have to educate your CPA, to whom the preceding may be a new concept.

**Generally Accepted
Accounting
Principles**

Only in recent years has the accounting profession given serious consideration to the accounting problems of nonprofit organizations. The American Institute of Certified Public Accountants (AICPA) and the Financial Accounting Standards Board (FASB) are responsible for setting accounting standards. In their *Statement of Accounting Concepts,* FASB does recognize that accounting for nonprofit organizations is different than accounting for profit-making ones. The AICPA has issued several audit guides[3] applicable to nonprofit organizations. At present, these guides recognize that the nature and extent of donated time and materials may be important. But, "because it is difficult to place a monetary value" on such voluntary contributions, it is accepted practice for accountants not to record them. Typically, CPAs include a footnote to financial statements of nonprofits that reads something like this:

> *No amounts have been reflected for donated services, since no objective basis is available to measure the value of such services. Nevertheless, a large number of volunteers have given significant amounts of their time to the organization's programs, fundraising campaigns, and management.*

One national nonprofit organization whose financial statements contain exactly such a footnote states in the text of its annual report that it benefitted from "the donated time of tens of thousands of volunteers."

I have already suggested that it *is* possible to measure, on an objective basis, the value of such services. It requires keeping records. This may be a difficult job, particularly at first, but it can be done. All of this is circular. Too many nonprofits do not keep accurate records of volunteer time and make little attempt to assign a dollar value to such time. CPAs have accepted this without questioning the validity of this omission or suggesting possible approaches to better documentation. This, in turn, validates the attitudes of the nonprofits. Someone has to break this cycle!

In order for you to discuss this with your CPA, it is important to know what the audit guides say. In general, they are all consistent in their treatment of donated time and materials. However, it appears that CPAs are not current in their understanding of good volunteer management practices as presented throughout this book. It will therefore be up to you to demonstrate that volunteers in your organization meet the stipulated criteria to be recorded in your financial records. Here is the language in the most recent guide:

> *The nature and extent of donated or contributed services received by organizations vary and range from the limited participation of many individuals in fund-raising activities to active participation in the organization's service program. Because it is difficult to place a monetary value on such services, their values are usually not recorded. The accounting standards division believes that those services should not be recorded as an expense, with an equivalent amount recorded as contributions or support, unless all of the following circumstances exist:*
>
> *a. The services performed are significant and form an integral part of the efforts of the organization as it is presently constituted; the services would be performed by salaried personnel if donated or contributed services were not available for the organization to accomplish its purpose; and the organization would continue this program or activity.*

b. *The organization controls the employment and duties of the service donors. The organization is able to influence their activities in a way comparable to the control it would exercise over employees with similar responsibilities. This includes control over time, location, nature, and performance of donated or contributed services.*

c. *The organization has a clearly measurable basis for the amount to be recorded.*

d. *The services of the reporting organization are not principally intended for the benefit of its members. Accordingly, donated and contributed services would not normally be recorded by organizations such as religious communities, professional and trade associations, labor unions, political parties, fraternal organizations, and social and country clubs.*[4]

It then goes on to say:

Participation of volunteers in philanthropic activities generally does not meet the foregoing criteria because there is no effective employer-employee relationship.[5]

Philosophically, I suggest the CPAs are incorrect. A well-managed volunteer program establishes the same relationship as the employer-employee relationship. Refer back to Chapter 9 and see this concept presented from a legal perspective. While there may be some question about "control" of time and duties of those volunteers engaged in certain types of fundraising activities, or perhaps of those volunteers who come to your agency as part of an already-established community group, most of the volunteer assignments considered in this book would be covered by the various criteria just outlined.

Donated Materials   Donated materials and facilities also have a dollar value and should be recorded. However, again, the audit guides do not make this easy to do:

Donated materials and facilities, if significant in amount, should be recorded at their fair value, provided the organization has a clearly measurable and objective basis for determining the value. If the materials are such that values cannot reasonably be determined, such as clothing, furniture, and so forth, which vary greatly in value depending on condition and style, they should not be recorded as contributions. If donated materials pass through the organization to its charitable beneficiaries, and the organization serves only as an agent for the donors, the donation should not be recorded as a contribution. The recorded value of the use of contributed facilities should be included as revenue and expense during the period of use.[6]

The important word here is "significant." If your organization receives donated materials or facilities and they are significant to your program, record them on your books. As you might guess, the definition of "significant" is not easy. I suggest the following guideline: if, in describing your program, leaving out a specific element would be a distortion, confuse your explanation or be misleading, then that specific element is "significant."

Many nonprofit organizations tell business people about the tax advantages of contributing inventory or items held for ordinary sale to a charitable organization. Technically this is correct. A corporation may deduct its basis (tax accounting jargon for "cost") for the contributed property plus one-half of the property's appreciated value (that is, market value), but the deduction cannot exceed twice the property's basis (cost). The actual paragraph from the tax code is really much more complicated, but I have exerpted it. For most donations, a business will deduct its inventory cost, the same value as if they threw the item away. Interestingly, if you record the value of the item as a contribution, you should use the *selling price* (fair market value), because that is the amount "it saved you."

The sample financial statements in this chapter were limited to showing donated services. Donated materials used in operations would be handled in exactly the same way as donated services. Under "Support and Revenue," the value of donated materials would be shown on a separate line. Similarly, they would be shown in the Statement of Functional Expenses, immediately following the cash expense for each particular cost element.

An additional rationale for making the effort to document and value donated materials is for budget preparation. If, for example, this year your organization receives $1,400 in donated light bulbs and you do not record this, at the time you prepare next year's budget, nothing may be included in the maintenance line item for light bulbs. If this turns out to be a one-time contribution, you have under-budgeted an expense that will have to be covered and have overlooked a dollar amount that must be included in your fundraising efforts.

Donated assets such as furniture and fixtures should be capitalized. The valuation of these and other types of donated items can be complicated and you should ask your accountant for advice.

The Internal Revenue Service

The IRS is ambivalent about what information it wants from nonprofit organizations. On the one hand, their Form 990, in Part VII ("Other Information"), asks the question: "Did your organization receive donated services or the use of materials, equipment or facilities at no charge or at substantially less than fair rental value?" If you answer "yes," there is a line on which you may indicate the value of such items. This means that the IRS recognizes the prevalence and importance of this type of donation to nonprofits, though it makes the reporting of such data optional.

On the other hand, there are clear instructions that the amount reported for donated services and materials may not be included elsewhere on the Form 990 as part of the organization's "support" or "expense." This perpetuates the concept that only transactions involving cash should be used in measuring the financial results of a nonprofit organization.

If you adopt the financial reporting system suggested in this chapter, it is a simple matter to pull out the figure of donated services and materials in order to complete the Form 990.

Tax Advantages to Volunteers

Volunteers should be informed that they can take certain deductions on their Federal income tax returns for some of the expenses incurred in their volunteer work. These contributions are all included as cash contributions on Schedule A for the volunteer's personal income tax return (Form 1040). For taxpayers who do not itemize, they are allowed to reduce their adjusted gross income by a percentage of their charitable contributions.

Basically, this means certain unreimbursed, out-of-pocket costs such as auto mileage (at 12¢ per mile under 1986 law); parking; tolls; train, bus or cab fares; travel expenses, lodging and meals for overnight trips; uniforms; telephone bills; office supplies; etc. Also, expenses spent *on* the service-user are deductible. For example, a Big Sister who takes her Little Sister to the zoo may deduct the admission price for her Little Sister—but *not* for herself.

Other items that are not deductible include the value of time donated (at *any* hourly rate), child care expenses, and meals (unless the volunteer is away overnight).

Your organization may, of course, reimburse volunteers for any expenses they incur on your behalf. Such reimbursement is not considered "income" to them for tax purposes.

Therefore, it makes sense that if a volunteer spends money for you and is not reimbursed, they have made a "contribution" to your organization. If you ask your volunteers to keep track of the items on which they spend money and give you a copy of their listing, there are benefits to both of you. You help them to keep records of possible Federal income tax deductions they might otherwise overlook. And you have documentation for recording these amounts as contributions to your organization.

Tickets purchased for fundraising events may be partially tax deductible. Any amount over the intrinsic value of the prize or event is deductible. For instance, a $50 special event ticket that includes dinner/entertainment worth $15 is deductible only in the amount of $35. This tax information should be shared with anyone who purchases a ticket.

The Value of Personal Services

As mentioned briefly above, the value of personal service given to a charitable organization is not deductible by an individual volunteer as a contribution. This is true whether the volunteer is self-employed or works for a company. In many cases, companies allow employees to do charitable work on company time, while on salary. This would usually be deductible *by the company* as an operating salary expense, but not as a contribution, unless the amount becomes significant enough to warrant other treatment.

Sometimes an individual will suggest giving your organization an invoice for hours worked and donated. This sounds fine, but upon closer examination has no benefit to either party and, in fact, can cause a tax liability to the individual volunteer.

If you do want to try this idea, your organization should record the "volunteer's" invoice as an *expense,* whether actually paid or not. If the invoice is cancelled, it should also be recorded as a *contribution.* If it is paid, but the payment is then given back to your organization, the same amount is a contribution. (This is similar to the above discussion of recording the value of volunteer time.)

For the "volunteer" in this transaction, s/he would need to record the invoice as *"income"* but would also have the *contribution* "expense"—and the net result would be zero. But, some taxes are based on gross receipts (billings). So the volunteer would be taxed on the value of the invoice, regardless of what s/he then chose to do with the money. Also, a corporation might have a loss and therefore not be able to deduct the contribution in the year it was made. In neither case is much gained.

However, some volunteers (those who are contributing their professional services) may want to prepare an invoice, giving a dollar amount for the services rendered, but marked with some appropriate wording such as "cancelled—contributed time." This invoice, needing no payment from the organization, provides a basis for the amount to be recorded as donated services. Legally, the volunteers do not have to record the cancelled invoice on their financial records, but the invoice gives them some documentation of their time.

There is also the variation of receiving a discount price for services. At the time of invoicing, you might request that the bill show the full, fair market value of the services, as well as the reduced fee. In this way you establish a more accurate base for your future budgeting and fundraising purposes. Of course, the discounted difference should be recorded on your financial records as a contribution.

As executive director, you must have a complete understanding of the financial aspects of your program. The procedures described in **It's Up to You**

this chapter will help you achieve this goal. Only with a total picture of your organization's resources and how they are used can you adequately explain them to your board and potential funders. This knowledge is also needed to manage your organization on a day-to-day basis.

1 Susan J. Ellis and Katherine H. Noyes, *Proof Positive: Developing Effective Volunteer Recordkeeping Systems,* Philadelphia: Energize Books, 1980.

2 G. Neil Karn, "The True Dollar Value of Volunteers," *The Journal of Volunteer Administration,* Vol. I, No. 2 (Winter 1982-83), pp. 1–17, and Vol. I, No.3 (Spring 1983), pp. 1–19.

3 The following are published by the American Institute of Certified Public Accountants:

Hospital Audit Guide (1972)
Audits of Colleges and Universities (1973)
Audits of Voluntary Health and Welfare Organizations (1974)
Audits of State and Local Governmental Units (1974)
Audits of Certain Nonprofit Organizations (1981)

The last guide listed was published to cover all nonprofit organizations not covered in the previously-issued guides.

4 American Institute of Certified Public Accountants, *Audits of Certain Nonprofit Organizations,* New York, 1981, pp. 77–8.

5 *Ibid.,* p. 78.
6 *Ibid.,* p. 79.

.

EXECUTIVE ROLE CHECKLIST

On a daily basis, the top executive has an important role in demonstrating support for the volunteer program within the organization s/he runs. The following is a summary of the basic elements of a successful volunteer program. Each element is described briefly, followed by a very specific set of responsibilities that belong to you—as the top executive—regardless of whom you have actually designated as head of the volunteer program. These are actions that require your leadership and authority.

You can use this as a checklist to assess your present level of participation in your organization's volunteer program . . . and to set goals for your future involvement in assuring the success of volunteers.

1. Planning

Planning is the key to success in all administrative responsibilities and volunteer management is no exception. Planning for volunteers involves the need to determine: exactly why volunteers are wanted; exactly what volunteers are expected to do; what resources will be necessary to support the work of volunteers; who will be designated to lead the volunteer effort; who will provide training and ongoing supervision of volunteers; and what preparation these key people will need.

EXECUTIVE ROLE:

☐ Develop the goals and objectives, and then the policies and procedures for volunteer involvement. Write and disseminate a "Statement of Philosophy" regarding volunteers.

☐ Staff the volunteer program appropriately.

☐ Budget funds and allocate other resources appropriately.

☐ Make sure that all salaried staff are trained to work effectively with volunteers and participate in identifying categories of work for volunteers.

☐ Include the director of volunteers in future planning for the organization.

☐ Allow volunteers to experiment for you by testing new ideas that may later be fundable.

2. Volunteer Job Descriptions

If an assignment cannot be described in writing, it probably is not a job. To assure effective utilization of volunteers, define the work to be done as specifically as possible. Volunteer job descriptions should, at a minimum, define: a title for the position; the purpose/rationale for the position; the scope of the work to be done (giving both the potential and limits of the job); the plan for training and supervision/collaboration; and the necessary time-frames. It is also important to determine how many hours of work will be needed to fulfill the function—not how many people (since volunteers have varied work schedules).

EXECUTIVE ROLE:

☐ Insist on having volunteer job descriptions put in writing.

☐ Make sure every unit and every administrative level in the organization submits requests for volunteers.

☐ Uphold the director of volunteers when s/he says "no" to an inappropriate request for volunteers.

☐ Develop job descriptions for volunteers to assist you directly, to model your personal acceptance of volunteer talents.

3. Recruitment/Public Relations

"Public relations" is what makes an organization visible to the public. It is necessary to have visibility and a good image so that people might consider volunteering for you. "Recruitment" is the process of encouraging people to give their time and energy to your organization. The best recruitment is targeted to the audiences most likely to have the skills and interests to match the available volunteer job descriptions.

EXECUTIVE ROLE:

☐ Be sure that the volunteer program (and therefore the opportunity to apply to become a volunteer) is mentioned in agency descriptive materials.

☐ Keep the director of volunteers informed of your speaking schedule and distribute volunteer recruitment materials whenever you distribute other agency literature.

☐ Invite the director of volunteers to accompany you to community events at which recruitment might be possible.

4. Screening and Selection

Many supervision and management problems can be prevented by effective initial interviewing of prospective volunteers. The screening (including screening out, if necessary) and selection process surfaces the expectations of the applicant and allows the director of volunteers to explain the standards of the organization. Also, each new volunteer should be matched to the most appropriate assignment.

EXECUTIVE ROLE:

☐ Back up the director of volunteer's right to screen out inappropriate candidates.

☐ Do not expect the director of volunteers to accept people as volunteers just because they are related to or referred by other salaried staff, board members, funders, etc.

☐ Do not let the Personnel Department send rejected job applicants to the Volunteer Office with the suggestion that volunteering is an alternative to employment with you.

☐ Apply the same hiring procedures and standards to volunteers as to employees.

5. Orientation

Orientation is the overview of the total organization necessary for every new volunteer, regardless of specific assignment. It places the work into context and allows for consistent introduction of policies, procedures, rights, and responsibilities.

EXECUTIVE ROLE:

☐ Participate in the welcoming of new volunteers (either in person each time, through videotape, or by a letter of greeting).

☐ Review the content of the orientation to be sure it represents the agency as you wish it to.

6. Volunteer Training

Training is individualized and should vary with the demands of each specific volunteer job description and the background each volunteer brings to the organization. There is the need for initial, start-up training, plus the need for ongoing, in-service training. Much "training" is really the giving of good instructions and is often integrated into the overall supervision plan.

EXECUTIVE ROLE:

☐ Recognize that it will take staff time to train volunteers and adjust work load demands accordingly.

☐ Develop a training plan for volunteers assigned directly to you.

7. Supervision of Volunteers

As with salaried staff, volunteer staff need support from those in a position to see the total picture and who know what work needs to be done. For volunteers, however, a key aspect of supervision is access to someone in charge during the actual time the volunteer is on duty or when the volunteer who is working independently in the field needs a question answered.

EXECUTIVE ROLE:

☐ Again, recognize that it will take staff time to supervise volunteers well.

☐ Clarify that volunteers are the responsibility of all staff members—and that volunteers do not "belong" to the director of volunteers.

☐ Include volunteers on the organizational chart under each unit in which they are active.

☐ Supervise the director of volunteers appropriately, or see to it that s/he answers to the most logical administrator. Regardless of who actually supervises the leader of the volunteer program, make yourself accessible if and when special questions needing decision-making authority arise concerning the involvement of volunteers.

☐ Reserve time to supervise volunteers assigned directly to you.

8. Recognition

Recognition is one way we "pay" volunteers for their efforts, but it has many nuances. If there is an annual banquet, but no daily support, recognition is given "with forked tongue"! While formalized, annual thank-you events are worthwhile, informal, continuous recognition is more important. This includes everything from simple courtesy to including volunteers in staff meetings and decision-making. It is also a part of recognition to offer constructive criticism, since such training implies a belief that the volunteer can do even better work.

EXECUTIVE ROLE:

☐ Be visible to volunteers year round and take time to interact with them occasionally in an informal manner.

☐ Participate in formal recognition events, whether as a speaker, in signing certificates, or by simply taking part.

☐ Periodically share updates on new agency developments, future plans, etc.—especially those that will affect volunteers.

☐ Provide visible recognition to salaried staff who have been successful in working with volunteers.

9. Coordination

By definition, volunteers are part-time staff. A volunteer program can have people who work once a year or regularly on schedules ranging from one afternoon a week to four days a week; mornings and evenings; alternate Sundays; etc. Add to this the diversity of the people who volunteer (all ages, backgrounds, physical conditions, academic degrees), and you end up with an amazing logistical challenge. A volunteer program must have a leader—and leadership includes coordinating all the details of scheduling and assigning.

EXECUTIVE ROLE:

☐ Recognize the unique nature of the volunteer scheduling pattern (diverse part-time hours) and make sure agency services can respond. For example, assure that the switchboard recognizes its important role in taking messages when the director of volunteers is unavailable, or keep evening reception desk staff informed about volunteer projects underway in the evenings.

☐ Assign adequate staff leadership to the volunteer program. At a minimum, designate evening, night or weekend supervisors responsible in the absence of the director of volunteers.

10. Recordkeeping and Reporting

If volunteers are important to the work of the organization, then it is important to know what volunteers are doing. Such documentation assists in recruitment, training, recognition, and fundraising. For purposes of insurance and to back up the income tax deduction claims of volunteers, recordkeeping by the agency is also vital. Once records are kept, they are of little meaning if they are not reported. Reports of the cumulative achievements of volunteers should be shared routinely with the volunteers themselves, as well as with top administration and funding sources.

EXECUTIVE ROLE:

☐ Expect to receive useful reports from the director of volunteers.

☐ Read and react to reports when submitted.

☐ Provide access to computer systems when possible and insist that the agency's computer programmers work with the director of volunteers to make the computer program do what is necessary to manage volunteers better.

☐ Make sure each department submits forms and other necessary data about volunteers to the volunteer office in a timely and complete fashion.

☐ Look for (and ask for) mention of volunteer activities in the reports of other department heads or staff members.

☐ Include data on the volunteer program in reports you make to the board or to funders. Also include such data in agency annual reports.

11. Evaluation

It is sinful to waste the time of a volunteer. Therefore it is imperative that volunteer programs regularly evaluate the impact of services performed and whether those services are still necessary. Along with program evaluation, it is helpful to conduct individual performance reviews with volunteers, so as to maintain motivation, troubleshoot potential problem areas, and allow for personal growth.

EXECUTIVE ROLE:

☐ Insist on performance—hold the volunteers to meeting goals and being productive.

☐ Include assessment of the volunteer program in any agency evaluation.

☐ Evaluate salaried staff on the criterion of how well they have worked with volunteers during the period being assessed.

☐ Ask volunteers for their perspective, opinions, and suggestions on the operational effectiveness of the organization.

12. Volunteer/Salaried Staff Relations

The interrelationship of volunteers and salaried staff is the single biggest pitfall, unless steps are taken early to encourage teamwork. There are numerous reasons why salaried staff are threatened by volunteers or why volunteers may be resistant to working well with employees. This is a human relations issue with no easy answers, but it should be remembered that almost no professional/academic training program prepares salaried staff to work with volunteers. So staff development training on this topic is vital. Clarification of roles and commitment from top administration are critical aspects to success in this area.

EXECUTIVE ROLE:

☐ Provide training for employees on the subject of working with volunteers successfully.

☐ Monitor the degree of acceptance of volunteers by the salaried staff. Provide positive and negative sanctions for working or not working well with volunteers.

☐ Include questions about past experience working with volunteers and being a volunteer on agency employment application forms/interviews.

☐ Include "supervision of volunteers" in the job description of any staff member who will be working with volunteers.

☐ Approach specific interpersonal problems between members of staff and particular volunteers objectively. Do not tip the scales in favor of the employee before hearing all the facts and be open to deciding that the volunteer may be right.

☐ Negotiate with union leaders as an advocate for volunteers.

13. Volunteer Input

Too many organizations want help, not input. Volunteers are in a position to observe the organization and can take more risks in criticizing or speaking out—which includes becoming effective advocates when things are going well. There must be a channel for such input or volunteers will either cause friction or leave. Also, defining a way for volunteers to voice opinions develops their ownership of the volunteer program.

EXECUTIVE ROLE:

☐ Develop channels for allowing volunteers to voice ideas and suggestions, including criticisms.

☐ Be open to considering volunteers' ideas.

☐ Respond to such ideas, even if you must explain why the suggestion cannot be implemented.

☐ Utilize volunteers to form collaborations between your and other organizations if jurisdictional lines are awkward.

☐ Maximize the special/unique benefits of volunteers on a day-to-day basis: use volunteers as a soundingboard and ask them to give you honest reactions to plans; tap their knowledge of the community; inform them of pending legislation affecting your cause and encourage them to contact community leaders or press their neighbors to vote; etc.

☐ Be accessible to meeting with volunteers personally when appropriate.

CONCLUSION

Historically, volunteers were the pioneers, the innovators who recognized existing community needs and found ways to meet them. Almost every institution and profession we take for granted today owes its initial establishment to the efforts of citizens who chose to become involved in a cause. Such pioneering continues to be a part of the volunteer picture today. In the last decade we have seen volunteers institute hospice programs, services to victims of abuse, and projects looking ahead to space colonization—just to name a few. The organization you head may well be able to name the key volunteers who filed your incorporation papers and made up your first board. Some of them may even still be around to see the fruits of their early labor.

The media gravitates towards labels such as "the me generation" or "self-involved Yuppies." Volunteering is the antithesis of such negative images. All the studies and polls prove that the vast majority of Americans do become involved in their communities. In fact, volunteering is so pervasive, we tend to take it for granted.

Recently legislative and economic changes have created uncertainty for many nonprofit organizations and government services. Volunteering has been tossed into the limelight, often for the wrong reasons. The question is not whether volunteers can fill budget gaps, but whether organizations are truly prepared to utilize volunteers in teamwork with salaried staff.

From the Top Down presents executives with the challenge of tapping community resources to the maximum. Volunteers cannot fully and successfully contribute to an organization unless they receive visibility and management attention. You have the authority and power necessary to set the tone for volunteer involvement in your organization—your vision and commitment will provide leadership for salaried and volunteer staff alike.

APPENDIX

VOLUNTEER MANAGEMENT/TASK ANALYSIS

The following detailed analysis of the role of the leader of a volunteer program first appeared in *No Excuses: The Team Approach to Volunteer Management by* Susan J. Ellis and Katherine H. Noyes (Energize Books) in 1981. It is still the only close examination of the scope of volunteer management and is reprinted here to give you a basis on which to write a job description for your leader of volunteers.

How to Use This Task Analysis:

1. The *functions* designated by Roman numerals and printed all in capital letters are the major areas of the job.

2. The *responsibilities* outlined A, B, C, etc. are the key activities in each function (what would usually appear in a regular job description).

3. The *tasks* listed in italics under each responsibility as 1, 2, 3, etc. are just some of the basic steps necessary to accomplish each responsibility. It is precisely these tasks that need to be identified both to *understand the job* and to select *assignments to delegate* to those who will help the director of volunteers.

4. This is a generalized Task Analysis. Details will vary from organization to organization. Therefore, space has been left throughout for you to make your own additions.

I. PROGRAM PLANNING AND ADMINISTRATION

A. Assess/analyze agency and client needs for assistance.
   1. *Design questionnaires, survey forms, etc. to deter-mine areas where assistance is needed.*
   2. *Interview (or otherwise contact) salaried staff, administration, volunteers, clients/consumers, etc.*
   3. *Tabulate results of interviews/surveys; summarize findings for agency personnel.*
   4. *Research models of other volunteer programs in similar settings.*

B. Develop program goals and objectives.
   1. *Determine possible long-range and short-range program goals, using data from the needs assessment.*
   2. *Review these with administration.*
   3. *Set timetable for implementation.*

C. Design volunteer assignments.
   1. *Determine job categories based on needs assessment and program goals.*
   2. *Write specific volunteer job descriptions.*
   3. *Review and revise job descriptions with appropriate salaried staff.*
   4. *Review set of job descriptions periodically with volunteers carrying those responsibilities, and revise as necessary.*
   5. *Write function descriptions for committees and organized groups in the volunteer program.*
   6. *Define the role of program advisors.*

D. Coordinate schedules.
   1. *Plan overall work schedule for volunteer assignments.*
   2. *Coordinate with salaried staff as needed.*
   3. *Follow attendance patterns with sign-in sheets and other systems of monitoring volunteer service. (See Function VIII)*

E. Set policies and procedures.
   1. *Review agency policies and procedures; consult*

with administration and supervisory staff about any requirements and rules affecting volunteers.

2. Determine overall volunteer program policies and procedures in conjunction with organizational decision-makers.

3. Determine policies and procedures for specific volunteer assignments.

4. Develop and maintain a volunteer program procedures manual.

F. Control budget.

1. Determine annual budget needs and convey them to administration.

2. Authorize budget expenditures.

3. Develop a petty cash system, a system for reimbursing volunteers, and any other necessary fiscal procedures.

4. Solicit in-kind donations for the volunteer program.

5. Plan and implement fundraising events for the volunteer program.

G. Manage operations.

1. Arrange for adequate space, furniture, equipment and supplies to support the volunteers.

2. Meet with supervisory staff to determine where (space) volunteers will work.

3. Order uniforms, nametags, etc., as appropriate; develop distribution system.

4. Develop transportation systems, day care options, etc.

H. Advocate for volunteers.

1. Inform agency staff about issues related to volunteers, especially such as insurance coverage, tax deductions, enabling funds, etc.

2. Initiate action on such issues, both within the organization and in support of community efforts, legislation, etc.

3. Represent the volunteers' point of view to the organization.

I.   Develop new projects.

     1. Participate in agency-wide program planning to assure proper involvement of volunteers from the start.

     2. Gather ideas for new volunteer projects and program expansion.

     3. Propose and justify such ideas.

     4. Initiate pilot projects to test ideas.

     5. Participate in related resource development and funding activities.

J.   Self-development.

     1. Subscribe and read professional volunteerism journals.

     2. Attend volunteer management workshops and conferences.

     3. Network with other directors of volunteers through local DOVIAs and VACs, and through national associations.

K.   Other:

II. RECRUITMENT AND PUBLIC RELATIONS

A.   Plan recruitment strategies.

     1. Identify the types of volunteers and/or skills needed for each volunteer job.

     2. Brainstorm (and then prioritize) available sources of potential volunteers.

     3. Solicit suggestions and contacts from salaried staff, present and past volunteers, family and friends, consumers, etc.

     4. Set up outreach objectives.

     5. Train assistant recruiters.

B.   Develop recruitment and media relations materials.
  1. *Design graphics and wording for flyers, posters, brochures, etc.*
  2. *Arrange to have these printed.*
  3. *Write and schedule (request) public service announcements on radio and television.*
  4. *Write and send press releases.*
  5. *Distribute/post materials at appropriate public sites.*
  6. *Develop slide shows and other audio-visual materials to support presentations.*

C.   Handle public speaking and personal contacts.
  1. *Contact leaders of groups of potential volunteers and arrange to speak to members.*
  2. *Accept speaking engagements requested by community groups.*
  3. *Seek out and do local radio, television and newspaper interviews and talk shows.*
  4. *Explain program needs in one-to-one meetings with key resource people.*
  5. *Develop corps of "program representatives" trained to speak on behalf of the program.*

D.   Manage ongoing recruitment efforts.
  1. *Maintain regular contact with frequent sources of volunteers (e.g., schools, churches, civic groups).*
  2. *Work with staff to insure that all agency public relations includes mention of volunteer opportunities.*
  3. *Distribute sets of recruitment materials to salaried staff and present volunteers, enlisting their help in locating new volunteers.*

E.   Other:

III. INTERVIEWING AND SCREENING

A.   Prepare for applicants.
    1. Design application form to be used by all prospective volunteers.
    2. Develop interview format appropriate to staff schedules, program setting and agency needs.
    3. Brief switchboard, receptionists, and secretaries that members of the public will be calling and coming in for appointments.

B.   Conduct interviews.
    1. Schedule interviews with all prospective volunteers.
    2. Obtain and review completed application forms.
    3. Describe various volunteer opportunities, using job descriptions.

C.   Screen.
    1. Screen out candidates inappropriate for the organization or having skills that could be better used in another setting by referring such applicants to other community volunteer programs.
    2. Adapt job descriptions to unique skills of prospective volunteers.
    3. Create special assignments when feasible.
    4. Develop procedures for accepting an applicant conditionally (such as a probationary period), if not certain as to her/his appropriateness.

D.   Make assignments.
    1. Tentatively match appropriate applicants to currently available assignments and schedule slots.
    2. Arrange for further screening, if necessary, by immediate supervisors of the assignment being considered.
    3. Make final decision to accept and schedule starting date.

E.   Deal with group volunteer involvement.
    1. Identify potential projects/assignments for organized groups of volunteers to handle independently.

   2. Meet with leaders of prospective groups of volun-
    teers and speak with members.
   3. Establish written guidelines for supervising work
    and liaisoning.

  F. Other:

IV. ORIENTATION AND TRAINING

  A. Develop an orientation program for all volunteers, regardless of assignment.
   1. Plan agenda.
   2. Arrange for tour of facility.
   3. Invite speakers (including key salaried staff, administration, board).
   4. Prepare informational materials to distribute to new volunteers.
   5. Schedule and conduct sessions as needed.
   6. Design individually-tailored orientation for specialized (one-shot or short-term) events or projects.
   7. Offer orientation to group volunteers at one of their meetings.

  B. Offer staff development.
   1. Identify level of expertise among salaried staff in working with volunteers; identify positive attitudes and negative attitudes.
   2. Meet individually with any staff member resistant to volunteers, in an attempt to discuss the situation and resolve it.
   3. Offer periodic staff seminars on volunteer management.
   4. In staff meetings, report on volunteer program progress and concerns.
   5. Participate in the orientation of new salaried staff so that they learn about the organization's volunteers from the beginning.

C.   Design initial training plan.
   1. Work with supervisors to design specific training for each volunteer assignment.
   2. Assist with the scheduling of training.
   3. Monitor that each volunteer receives training.
   4. Develop and conduct initial training for volunteers directly working under volunteer office supervision.
   5. Involve experienced volunteers in assisting newcomers.

D.   Develop in-service training options.
   1. Solicit needs and interests in in-service training from volunteers and salaried staff; form in-service training program committee.
   2. Plan viable annual training schedule.
   3. Prepare for sessions; invite speakers and resource people.
   4. Possibly conduct sessions or moderate them.
   5. Evaluate training plan and results periodically.
   6. Explore possible ways to collaborate with other volunteer programs to offer additional in-service training.
   7. Arrange for volunteers to attend special events, workshops, tours, etc.

E.   Prepare manuals and handbooks.
   1. Gather information for inclusion in a manual.
   2. Review sample manuals from other programs.
   3. Discuss possible contents with volunteers and agency staff.
   4. Write manual.
   5. Design appearance and arrange for printing.
   6. Distribute copies to all appropriate persons.

F.   Other:

V. SUPERVISION

    A.   Handle direct supervision.

        1. Meet regularly/periodically with members of management team.

        2. Establish supervision plan for volunteers assigned directly to the volunteer office.

        3. Maintain regular contact (written and oral) with off-site volunteers and/or their supervisors.

    B.   Handle indirect supervision.

        1. Communicate regularly with those staff who directly supervise volunteers.

        2. Assure that volunteers are utilized appropriately, with tasks suited to their abilities.

        3. Check that supervisors are accessible to volunteers and are maintaining a regular schedule of supervisory contact.

    C.   Be a liaison.

        1. Serve as "third party" moderator to resolve any problems arising between volunteers and salaried staff members.

        2. If necessary, substitute as supervisor in absence of regular staff supervisor.

        3. Be available to all volunteers and salaried staff as next step in the "chain of command."

    D.   Maintain overall standards for volunteer performance and supervision.

    E.   Supervise salaried staff directly assigned to the volunteer program.

    F.   Other:

VI. MOTIVATION AND RECOGNITION

A. Assure ongoing volunteer motivation and appreciation.

   1. *Promote agency-wide atmosphere of welcome, courtesy, motivation and productivity.*
   2. *Help salaried staff demonstrate appreciation of volunteers on a day-to-day basis.*
   3. *Establish methods for volunteers to express concerns and offer suggestions.*
   4. *Act as advocate for volunteerism in general and for individual volunteers within the program.*
   5. *Promote communication among program participants through such devices as a program newsletter, bulletin boards, and staff meetings.*
      a) assign a newsletter editor
      b) plan publication schedule and format
      c) keep bulletin boards attractive and informational
      d) schedule periodic meetings for volunteers as an entire staff, or in clusters according to project, shift, etc.
   6. *Attend salaried staff meetings and report on program progress.*

B. Initiate formal, periodic recognition activities.

   1. *Plan formal recognition of all volunteer services.*
      a) schedule an event
      b) purchase or prepare tokens of appreciation
      c) arrange program
      d) plan refreshments; possibly deal with caterer
      e) send invitations and arrange publicity
   2. *Identify those volunteers eligible for special recognition.*
   3. *Also thank those salaried staff who contributed to the volunteer program.*
   4. *Write letters of reference for volunteers when requested.*
   5. *Involve top agency personnel in expressing appreciation.*

    C.   Develop "career ladders" for volunteers.

       1. Review all assignments regularly to see that volunteers continue to be challenged and enjoy their activities.

       2. Design advanced-level tasks for those volunteers earning and desiring more difficult (responsible, sophisticated) work.

       3. Utilize experienced volunteers in special projects, such as ad hoc committees, representing program at community meetings, etc.

       4. Utilize experienced volunteers in program evaluation and planning, and as trainers of new volunteers.

    D.   Other:

VII. EVALUATION

    A.   Conduct regular program evaluation.

       1. Develop a plan for program evaluation; form an evaluation team.

       2. Design questionnaires, surveys, etc.; recruit and train interviewers.

       3. Solicit input from all program constituents.

       4. Analyze data and develop concrete plan of action based on evaluation results.

       5. Report evaluation results to all program constituents.

    B.   Assess ongoing progress in all program components.

       1. Informally, keep informed about progress in all areas:

       a) ask questions

       b) meet with volunteers and staff

       c) evaluate methods during supervisory meetings.

2. *Track pilot projects carefully; review at scheduled intervals.*
3. *Conduct "exit interviews" with volunteers leaving the organization to gain insights into areas for improvements in assignments and management.*

C. Supervise individual volunteer performance assessment.
    1. *Develop a plan for periodic assessment of volunteers' progress, achievements, areas requiring further training, etc.*
    2. *Train supervisors to conduct periodic, mutual evaluations, in a constructive way, with all volunteers assigned to them.*
    3. *Review all such evaluative reports.*
    4. *Evaluate performance of volunteers assigned directly to the volunteer office.*
    5. *Insure that volunteers do self-evaluation and have opportunity to evaluate their training, supervision, etc.*

D. Other:

VIII. RECORDKEEPING AND REPORTING

A. Develop records system.
    1. *Determine data needs for program records.*
    2. *Review agency records and reporting systems, to see where volunteer data could mesh.*
    3. *Develop a comprehensive recordkeeping system to document full extent of the contributions/activities of volunteers.*
    4. *Design forms and develop procedures to gather data.*
    5. *Train volunteers and salaried staff to use forms properly.*

B.   Maintain system.
    1. Record data in an accurate, up-to-date and acces-
    sible manner.
    2. Monitor use of forms.
    3. Follow up forms or reports not turned in.
    4. Keep records on own activities as Director of
    Volunteers.

C.   Develop reports.
    1. Write monthly and annual reports, giving both sta-
    tistics and descriptive narratives.
    2. Distribute reports to all program constituents, as
    well as to administration.
    3. Prepare special reports upon request.

D.   Other:

IX. OTHER RESPONSIBILITIES

A.   Participate in agency fundraising events, coordinating
    volunteer assistance.

B.   Solicit in-kind donations to assist agency services.

C.   Represent the organization at community functions;
    represent the organization to visiting community
    members (give tours, etc.).

D.   Provide liaison with other volunteer efforts, such as
    board development, working with auxiliaries, etc.

E.   Other:

APPENDIX

VOLUNTEERISM RESOURCES

Volunteerism is growing as a distinct management discipline and volunteer administration is emerging as a profession. This means that the skills of developing and managing volunteers are being codified so that newcomers to this responsibility can learn from the experience of their predecessors. It should be noted that "volunteerism" is a different discipline than "voluntarism," despite the fact that these two words are often confused. Voluntarişm refers to all voluntary activities in a society (in the United States that includes religion, for example) and covers issues of concern to voluntary agencies. Volunteerism, on the other hand, refers to anything involving volunteers and volunteering, regardless of setting. Government agencies, which are not part of the "voluntary sector," may indeed be included under the umbrella of "volunteerism" when it comes to volunteers active in courts, parks and recreation, and all other such public services.

In most geographic areas it is increasingly possible to obtain some training in volunteer administration, either through a formal academic institution or through workshops sponsored by a wide array of organizations. Books and journals on volunteerism are available. Conferences for leaders of volunteer programs have also proliferated on both the state and national levels.

As executive, you should expect your director of volunteers to become familiar with such resources and to become active in relevant professional associations. It is important to encourage the director of volunteers to seek out colleagues in volunteerism generically, as well as those in settings similar to yours. Many of the approaches and techniques successfully utilized in other types of organizations can be applied with equal success in any setting.

If you do not already have a director of volunteers, you may need to become familiar with some volunteerism resources yourself, or help the staff member you have designated to work with volunteers part-time make use of such resources. To this end, here are some of the most commonly available places in which to seek information on volunteerism.

Voluntary Action Centers

Voluntary Action Centers, often referred to by their acronym of "VAC," are also called Volunteer Centers or Volunteer Bureaus in some cities. VACs act as clearinghouses for information on volunteer opportunities. Organizations seeking volunteers can "register" their needs, while members of the public can contact the VAC to discover what volunteer assignments are available.

Different VACs engage in different projects. Some publish a directory of local volunteer opportunities while others actually interview potential volunteers and try to individualize the assistance in finding the right volunteer job. Many VACs organize community-wide events for National Volunteer Week (occurring annually in April) or coordinate collaborative recruitment efforts such as shopping mall fairs. The larger VACs also maintain libraries of materials on volunteer program development.

If your community has a VAC, by all means get on its mailing list. This should assure you of receiving information about local training workshops, conferences, or meetings focused on volunteerism.

Because VACs are nonprofit institutions (many are funded through United Way), the majority of their services are offered free of charge or at low cost. It may even be possible to receive consultation from the VAC in how to start your volunteer program or in how to locate a director of volunteers.

DOVIAs

Whether or not your community has a VAC, it may have what has come to be called, generically, a "DOVIA." This stands for "Directors of Volunteers in Agencies" and is simply an association of people who have the responsibility for leading the volunteer program in their agencies. DOVIAs usually meet on a regular basis several times a year and operate as self-help groups. They plan their meetings to provide a mixture of collegial interaction (often the main benefit of attending) and provision of information. There is usually a speaker who addresses the group about some aspect of volunteer management.

The more established DOVIAs sponsor periodic workshops for which nationally-known trainers may be invited. Newsletters and other forms of resource exchange are also common. All costs for these activities are covered through membership dues or registration fees.

State Offices

More than half the States have a state-level office charged with coordinating volunteerism. Such offices have names that are some version of State Office on Voluntary Citizen Participation, Governor's Office on Volunteerism, etc. Their mandates range as widely as their names, but all attempt to be state-level clearinghouses of information about citizen involvement in their State. In some ways, State Offices function as VACs for a wider geographic area.

Again, be sure you are on the mailing list of your State Office, if you are lucky enough to be in a State that has one. The good State Offices sponsor statewide conferences for volunteer leaders and publish information newsletters.

State Associations

In some States, directors of volunteers have organized into professional associations on the state level. Such associations usually operate independently of any existing DOVIAs or VACs, though collaboration is common in planning conferences, etc. There is no pattern to whether state associations are strong where there is no State Office, or whether they are strong in support of a State Office.

National Resources

On the national level there are several organizations devoted to furthering volunteerism generically, as well as some focused on one or another specific field of voluntary action. The three major generic national organizations and their quarterly publications are:

—Association for Volunteer Administration *(The Journal of Volunteer Administration)*

—VOLUNTEER: The National Center *(Voluntary Action Leadership)*

—Association of Voluntary Action Scholars *(Journal of Voluntary Action Research)*

In addition, ACTION is the Federal agency responsible for carrying out national government-sponsored volunteer projects. Independent Sector also considers volunteering one of its focus areas.

For specific fields, here is a sampling of the national organizations active in 1986:

—American Society of Directors of Volunteer Services, of the American Hospital Association (limited to directors of volunteers in AHA-accredited hospitals). ASDVS has state affiliates in all states, with many of those having local chapters as well.

—National Association on Volunteers in Criminal Justice

—Accountants for the Public Interest

—National School Volunteer Program

—National Association of Museum Volunteers

Because of the changing nature of the field of volunteerism, this book does not give addresses for any of these organizations. When you are ready to seek out such networks, start by locating your local resources such as a VAC or DOVIA—or contact a director of volunteers in any major community agency.

Also a fluid category, at the time of
this writing there is at least one
insurance program specifically
developed to cover the unique
needs of a volunteer project: the Volunteer Insurance Service
(VIS). VIS is administered by Corporate Insurance Management in
Washington, D.C.

**Insurance
Resources**